Private Law

Friedrich Julius Stahl

THE PHILOSOPHY OF LAW

VOLUME I: *The History of Legal Philosophy*

1A: *The Rise and Fall of Natural Law*

1B: *The Recovery of Historical Law*

VOLUME II: *The Doctrine of Law and State on the Basis of the Christian Worldview*

PART I: *General Doctrines and Private Law*

BOOK I: *Philosophical Foundations*

BOOK II: *Principles of Law*

BOOK III: *Private Law*

PART II: *The Doctrine of State and the Principles of State Law*

BOOK IV

Private Law

The Philosophy of Law
Volume II: The Doctrine of Law and State on the Basis of the Christian Worldview
Book III
SECOND EDITION

Friedrich Julius Stahl

Translated, edited, and prefaced by
Ruben Alvarado

WORDBRIDGE PUBLISHING
Aalten, the Netherlands
www.wordbridge.net
info@wordbridge.net

German original: Friedrich Julius Stahl, *Rechts- und Staatslehre auf der Grundlage christlicher Weltanschauung: Erste Abtheilung, enthaltend die allgemeinen Lehren und das Privatrecht.* Third edition. Tübingen and Leipzig: J. C. B. Mohr, 1854.

ISBN 978–90–76660–78–3

COVER ILLUSTRATION: "The Judgment of Solomon" by Giorgione (c. 1500). This reproduction is courtesy of Wikimedia Commons and is in the public domain.

TABLE OF CONTENTS

NOTES ON THIS EDITION

The edition used for this translation is the 3rd edition of the *Philosophy of Law*, published by Mohr of Tübingen in 1854. Words in German which are susceptible to multiple meanings or the meaning of which was not totally clear have been left in the text in square brackets. Square brackets are also used to insert interpolations for understanding or to provide supplementary material. Section headings do not appear in the original: they are of my own device.

Numbers which appear in bold between two angular brackets (like this: **<1>**) are page numbers of the original edition. References in the text and in the indices to page numbers in this book refer to that page numbering.

Roman- and canon-legal terms are set off in the text with a boldface Roman font, e.g., **successio universalis**. An index of such terms is provided at the end of the book, along with the page numbers of their appearance. Many of these terms may be referenced in William Smith, *A Dictionary of Greek and Roman Antiquities* (URL: https://tinyurl.com/ 48au6euy).

A word about the word *Vermögen*. As explained in the text, this refers to "property in the broad sense" as opposed to *Eigentum*, property in the strict sense. As such, *Vermögen* is an umbrella term covering both property and contract. The origin of this legal concept lies in Roman law. In the Roman legal tradition, property and contract together form the "law of things." This law was further developed in the German legal tradition, in which the Roman concept of things became the concept of *Vermögen*, which roughly corresponds to "assets." Therefore, in the German tradition both property and contract are forms of assets. To indicate this distinction, we translate the word *Vermögen* as property* (with an asterisk).

Sections (parts of §§. 69, 70, and 76, along with §§. 77–79) left out of the first edition have been included in this second edition of *Private Law*. The text has been corrected where necessary and improved where appropriate.

GENERAL PREFACE TO "THE DOCTRINE OF LAW AND STATE ON THE BASIS OF THE CHRISTIAN WORLDVIEW"

<xi> Together with the *History of Legal Philosophy*, *The Doctrine of Law and State on the Basis of the Christian Worldview* comprises Friedrich Julius Stahl's magnum opus, *The Philosophy of Law.* This multivolume production provides us with the philosophical foundations upon which Stahl's career as a professor of constitutional law, as a parliamentarian, and as a statesman in 19th century Bavaria and Prussia was based.[1] It is also unique: it is the only comprehensive work of legal philosophy produced by a modern, post-French-Revolution conservative, to wit, a follower of the pioneer in this regard, Edmund Burke.

Conservatism has always been in need of such a comprehensive philosophical system. For opposition to the Revolution did not necessarily lead to unity of worldview. Many conservatives were Roman Catholic and hence argued for a return to (idealized) pre-revolutionary conditions in church and state, thus for the primacy of the monarchy and the papacy – these generally bore the name Counter-Revolutionary. Others were Protestant, and thus perceived a need to move beyond pre-revolutionary conditions, albeit in a manner which maintained continuity with the political, legal, and cultural inheritance of Europe. Among the latter group Stahl was pre-eminent; he was the first of the so-called Anti-Revolutionaries, who in the **<xii>** Netherlands even formed a political party under the leadership of Guillaume Groen van Prinsterer and Abraham Kuyper.

Stahl was a protege of Friedrich Carl von Savigny, himself the pioneer of the "Burkean" worldview in Germany. Savigny is best known for his argument against codification and in favor of legal continuity, including the primacy of customary law, as contained in his *On the Vocation of Our Age for Legislation and Legal Science.* Such arguments were completely in line with what Edmund Burke had argued in his *Reflections on the Revolution in France* and elsewhere. Savigny founded what came to be known as the Historical School of Juris-

[1] For more on Stahl's life see my *Authority Not Majority* (Aalten: WordBridge, 2007).

prudence, perhaps the most influential school of legal science Germany ever produced.

The problem with this school was that it lacked a solid grounding in legal philosophy. Writing in 1901, James Viscount Bryce, the noted legal historian and diplomat of late 19th-early 20th century Britain, claimed that in view of its methodology it is “more applicable to the law of any particular country than to the theory of law in general, for the details of legal history vary so much in different countries that immense knowledge and unusual architectonic power are needed to combine their general results for the purposes of a comprehensive theory” (*Studies in History and Jurisprudence*, II, p. 186). Indeed, Bryce considered the task so monumental that he doubted it had ever been done, though it “may be done, and so will doubtless be done some day. Everything happens at last.”

As a matter of fact, the task had long since been accomplished, even by someone “of the requisite capacity” as stipulated by Bryce.[2] In fact, Stahl had already published the first edition of his *The Doctrine of Law and State on the Basis of the Christian Worldview*, presenting a legal philosophy sprung from the loins of the Savignian historical method, back in the 1830s when he was a young law professor in Bavaria. Savigny recog- **<xiii>** nized it as providing the essential underpinnings in eternal verities that he himself had failed to produce.[3] And in providing this service, Stahl not only gave the Historical School a philosophical basis, he gave the Burkean common law school of thought a basis as well, although the Anglo-Saxon world of jurisprudence was unaware of it, then as now.

---

[2] For more on the curious ignorance of Stahl on the part of future generations, see the preface to G. Groen van Prinsterer, *In Memory of Stahl* (Aalten: Pantocrator Press, 2022).

[3] For an alternative interpretation of this development, see John E. Toews, “The Immanent Genesis and Transcendent Goal of Law: Savigny, Stahl, and the Ideology of the Christian German State,” *The American Journal of Comparative Law,* 37, no. 2 (Winter, 1989), 139–169; idem, *Becoming Historical: Cultural Reformation and Public Memory in Early Nineteenth-Century Berlin* (New York: Cambridge University Press, 2004), ch. 5: “The Tension Between Immanent and Transcendent Subjectivity in the Historical School of Law: From Savigny to Stahl.”

The English common law has never enjoyed the philosophical attention that has been lavished on Continental legal systems. The reason is of course its being a product of court practice without being made the continuous subject of scholarly analysis, as was done on the Continent. Even so, this did not preclude the development of a unique legal philosophy which, although it did not attain to the sophistication of Continental efforts, nevertheless developed into a full-fledged philosophical jurisprudence in its own right, inoculating the legal system from the challenge of natural-rights jurisprudence and enlightened-despot codification efforts the likes of which took over on the Continent during the 18th century Enlightenment. The common-law approach pioneered by Edward Coke, John Selden, and Matthew Hale (Coke and Hale were chief justices) provided the basis for Burke's political philosophy. And from this root came the Continental resurgence of conservatism, which had been driven out of business by Enlightenment rationalism.[4] **<xiv>**

Regardless of the success this approach had both in preserving English common-law traditions and in reinvigorating Continental common-law traditions, in terms of legal philosophy it remained rudimentary. William Blackstone's *Commentaries on the Laws of England* (1769), which served as target practice for Jeremy Bentham and his utilitarianism, is paradigmatic in this regard. Indeed, from Bentham onward it might be stated that utilitarianism and pragmatism have been the leading philosophical approaches for dealing with the common law (e.g., Oliver Wendell Holmes, Roscoe Pound). And that legacy lives on into the present day (as witness its latest iteration, "Law and Economics," as exemplified in the work of Richard Posner and Richard Epstein). The alternative is a natural- rights school of thought based essentially on John Locke and the *Declaration of Independence*, and which in consequence is constantly fighting a rear-guard action against French Revolutionary principles.[5]

It might seem anachronistic that help on this front would come, of all places, from pre-Bismarckian Germany. But the sense of anachronism fades when one realizes the affinity between the pre-Revolutionary Continental and English

---

[4] On this most interesting history, see Harold J. Berman, "The Origins of Historical Jurisprudence: Coke, Selden, Hale," *Yale Law Journal* 103, no. 7 (1994).

[5] For details on this see my *Trojan Horse: Natural Rights and America's Founding* (Aalten: WordBridge, 2022).

legal systems. It is the divergence between these two which is constantly emphasized; but how is it, then, that Burke could postulate a fundamental legal continuity across Western Europe which was only ruptured by the French Revolution?[6] Indeed, Savigny and his followers recognized in English common law a cognate legal system to the German pre-codification legal system. Which is what makes Stahl's legal philosophy so interesting to common-law legal science. Stahl provides principles applicable to the English common law as well as Continental law, for he draws upon the common inheritance of Western legal science such as described in part by Harold Berman in his *Law* **<xv>** *and Revolution,*[7] a legal science sharing essential characteristics, maintaining similar institutions, pursuing similar goals.

What Stahl does is provide an understanding of the solid, unchanging foundations to the evolving, adapting thing which is the common law. Considerations of utility and pragmatism are made subordinate to principles of justice and what he calls providential purposes, within the context of historical development. Burke's partnership "between those who are living, those who are dead, and those who are to be born"[8] finds a distinct echo here, as does his conceptualization of rights as inheritance rather than *a priori,* a-historical givens. Likewise, rights are made subordinate to law rather than being the source of law as conceived by the natural-rights school. What's more, Stahl provides subjective right with a clear position and demarcation within the legal system, which is a feat in itself and, perhaps more than anything else, is needed in today's confused, rights-bloated jurisprudence.

---

[6] "If diffident of yourselves, and not clearly discerning the almost obliterated constitution of your ancestors, you had looked to your neighbours in this land, who had kept alive the ancient principles and models of the old common law of Europe meliorated and adapted to its present state – by following wise examples you would have given new examples of wisdom to the world." Edmund Burke, *Reflections on the Revolution in France,* vol. 2 of *Select Works of Edmund Burke* (Indianapolis: Liberty Fund, 1999), p. 125.

[7] Harold J. Berman, *Law and Revolution: The Formation of the Western Legal Tradition* (Cambridge, ma: Harvard University Press, 1983).

[8] Burke, *Reflections,* p. 193.

The concept he uses to establish these foundations is that of a *doctrine* of law and state. In the introduction he provided to Volume II as a whole (see *Philosophical Foundations*, p. 1), Stahl explains this notion of doctrine: it is something other than jurisprudence on the one hand and legal philosophy on the other. Jurisprudence is the science of a particular legal system as it exists in a particular country at a particular time; legal philosophy is its opposite, bringing "law and state into connection with the highest cause and the final goal of all existence" (*Philosophical Foundations,* p. 2). The doctrine of law and state occupies an intermediate position. It generalizes from jurisprudence while it particularizes **<xvi>** from legal philosophy. It operates in terms of universals but fleshes out those universals in terms of the particulars provided by jurisprudence. In so doing it provides universal criteria out of which particular legal systems can be generated and by which they can be judged.

Stahl bases this doctrine of law and state on the Christian worldview: because historically the nations of Western civilization likewise were based on that worldview, and because every such universal doctrine must base itself on one worldview or another. "Every philosophical system of whatever name in the final analysis rests on a foundational presupposition that is nothing more than faith, no matter what claim it may make to so-called scientific certainty" (*Philosophical Foundations,* p. 3). So, ultimately Stahl provides us with a Christian common-law legal philosophy, in doing so epitomizing the Western legal tradition in its conservative variant.

PREFACE TO "PRIVATE LAW"

<xvii> This book is a translation of Book III of *The Doctrine of Law and State.* It provides Stahl's detailed outworking in private law of the principles of law developed in Book II, *Principles of Law.* "In accordance with the dual relation of human common life," it says there (§. 45, p. 119 in the original pagination), "legal relations are of two sorts. The one serves to satisfy the *individual person*, to complete his existence... the other serves to rule men collectively, to join them into a common existence and to complete it as such. The former make up *private law*, the latter *public law.*" Here follows, then, an elucidation of private law, the law as it relates to persons in their individual relations.

Permeating the work is the understanding of private law having a twofold basis, a rootedness in the natural creation – a givenness of nature determining all legal institutions – and the principle of personality acting within those creation givens, resulting in the institutions of private law. "Private law therefore springs from a dual principle: *the objective purpose* (τέλος) *of life relations* as grounded in the arrangement of nature... ; and the eternal *idea of personality* which, on the basis of the former, in the final analysis gives legal institutions their shape" (p. 2). This is the twofold basis of law developed by Stahl in *Principles of Law* (§§. 5, 7, 39, 40).

The starting point is the right of the person. This right of the person is the primeval, inalienable right, the basis of all further rights in civil society. It entails integrity, freedom, honor, legal capacity, and protection of acquired rights. This basic setup is inherent in each individual person; upon it is erected the positive rights which go into every separate civil constitution.

So then, "personality is the substrate of free action," the basis for the range of civil rights; but it does not itself contain that range of civil rights. The latter are positive, acquired through one's effort or that of one's forefathers, or are entered into as part of a greater institution, as for example entering into marriage puts one into the position of husband or wife, father **<xviii>** or mother, head of household, testator. In particular, far from establishing an equality of rank or property, it establishes the preconditions precisely for inequality in rank or property. For "*equality* is a primeval right of man, albeit in precise measure, according to a determinate relation. It does not rule out distinctions and rank, the inequality of actual rights, the inequality even of the capacity for rights. Abstract and unconditional equality ('égalité') is by no means a primeval right of man" (p. 22).

Freedom is likewise subject to misunderstanding. The modern concept of freedom is choice between good and evil, and the greater the range of choices available, the better. But this is not freedom at all. True freedom consists in the ability to choose the good and the right. Such a capacity is not just *there*, it must be fostered and conserved, and a just and free legal order recognizes that. "The first condition of legal freedom is thus the reasonableness of laws. The unreasonableness and thus immorality of laws is the first suppression of freedom. By contrast, the maintenance of a public life-order in the people and this order's restriction of our actions is not in itself a reduction of our freedom but rather a postulate of it. When this order truly is morally reasonable, it sets us not against our actual self but in accordance with it" (p. 16).

The modern viewpoint also has it that full humanity is the principle of all civil society, and that human rights are the fulfillment thereof. But it forgets that there is another principle of society, the fear of God, and that it is that principle, in its Christian form, which preceded the appearance of the principle of full humanity *and in fact engendered it.* Both principles are necessary to a healthy and just social order.

Following upon these basic considerations, the "meat" of the law is addressed, beginning with the institution of property. **<xix>**

In line with Stahl's understanding of legal institutions as combining creation imperatives with the higher calling of personality, he understands property as the means through which man expresses his personality. Things are the medium through which he does this, through which he gives shape to his life; and freedom is the necessary prerequisite for him to be able to accomplish that. Property then also serves an ethical purpose, in that through property man can fulfill ethical duties which otherwise he could not. "Therefore property is not simply the satisfaction of human self-interest or the necessary means of maintenance, nor is it merely the purposeless rule over things; it is the material and means for a vocation, and therefore is itself a vocation" (p. 44).

The community of goods short-circuits this vocation and therefore cannot be what it claims, a higher sort of ethical condition; the inequality of property is in fact the just outworking of a social order in which personality and freedom of expression are given free rein, and where God's providential ordering is respected.

In its origin, property is collective and it is landed. Nations, not individuals, take possession of the land, from whence it is parceled out. This forms the basis of all further forms of property. Although its origin lies in grant, such a grant is irrevocable; the further course of property-holding and exchange lies beyond the distributing hand of government. "In its initial origin, [property] is not grounded in one's own power but on authority, it is not something attained but something received. On the other hand, its independence begins immediately; the initial distribution is irrevocable, and upon this basis property is further acquired through the particular act and destiny of each individual" (p. 52). Furthermore, property in its origin is as original as is contract and the state. Therefore, to found property on contract, as the natural-rights theorists such <xx> as Grotius would have it, is as foolish as to found the state on contract.

Property involves two elements: satisfaction and control. Satisfaction is the purpose for which property exists: to provide for human needs and wants. Control is the indispensable means through which it attains to this purpose. Control is the means by which personality is injected into the workings of attainment of satisfaction.

Property can be construed broadly and narrowly. Property narrowly speaking is the absolute right to a certain material thing. But there is also property broadly speaking, which embraces all forms of entitlement. In German the term for this is *Vermögen;* as there is no English translation for this word, "property*" (with an asterisk) will have to suffice. For all forms of entitlement, including both partial rights to things, such as usufruct, and rights to the performances of persons – obligations – are likewise means of establishing control over media of satisfaction, thereby making one's world more secure, one's future more certain.

The Communist-Socialist repudiation of property, for its part, obliterates this plan of free personality working through things and performances; but most of all, it denies the reality of God's dispensation. "As is the case with all efforts at all times to achieve a community of goods, the error of Communism therefore consists in general in the denial of the ethical meaning of property and the illusion regarding the ethical value of the community of goods; but in particular it consists – and this is its innermost distinguishing characteristic – in the non-recognition of the leading of God in the distribution of goods" (p. 64).

In line with the two main forms of property* (i.e., in the broad sense) described above, the law of property* is divided into two main forms of rights: real and personal. Real rights **<xxi>** are rights to things; personal rights are rights to performances by others. (Personal rights are not to be confused with the right of the person as discussed above.)

Real rights are those which establish control over a thing, where "the thing must serve one person fully and completely as the object of his will, so that he freely disposes over it" (p. 71). The most complete control is property in the strict sense; but particular powers can be fragmented and made into partial rights, such as easements, servitudes, usufructs, liens, leases, and the like. Joint ownership is also possible, with Germanic law providing better forms than Roman. Acquisition of property occurs in two main ways: original and derivative. Original acquisition is gained where ownership did not previously obtain; derivative acquisition occurs where ownership is assumed from a previous owner. A form of real right which does not attain to the status of property is possession: this is merely protection in a factual state of affairs, in which one has physical possession of a certain thing; the law requires that this factual condition be preserved even where title is lacking.

Personal rights establish, in line with their character as property*, control over the performance of another. "Performances [Leistungen] by other people serve the needs of our existence just as much as does the possession of things, and the activity of personality in freely giving shape to the way of life, which requires property in things, therefore also requires the same power of free disposal and the same enduring secure right over that other means of existence" (p. 95). These personal rights are called obligations. Their significance lies "not so much [in making] possible services or the communication of things – this can be achieved by mere factual performance – but much rather that security of the future exist, partly by making possible a present performance or communication... without damage and hazard, and partly through which the future **<xxii>** possession of an object is secured in a manner often not afforded even by continuous possession" (p. 95).

In accordance with the nature of property* as being an affair of freedom, two basic forms of personal right exist, categorized in terms of the role of the will in them: contract, engaged voluntarily, and tort, engaged involuntarily. Contract is "a mutual stated agreement among specific persons regarding a legal relationship to be founded amongst themselves" (p. 100). It has two forms. The one establishes relations the continued existence of which is independent of this contract, as for example marriage; the other contains within itself both the foundation and continued content of the relation, "so that complete fulfillment continuously proceeds only in pursuance of the agreement and according to the standard it sets.... The former are contractual *acts*, the latter contractual *relations*, that is to say, the former arise through contract (agreement) without themselves being contracts" (p. 101). This underscores the importance but also the subordinate character of contract. Just because a relationship is established by contract does not mean that its content is freely to be determined: this is especially important in the understanding of marriage. And vice versa, contract can serve as a true source of law where its contents are legally valid; by it, the agreeing parties may set up for themselves various legally binding arrangements which serve as a law for them.

The law of the family follows the law of property*. Here as well, the key factors are the forces of the natural creation being harnessed to the exigencies of personality and freedom.

> Solely by virtue of the personality of man, these relationships, which in the lower reaches of creation only form momentary passing acts, with him becoming enduring bonds permeating all of existence. The complement of the sexes becomes a bond of imperishable full personal devotion, be- **<xxiii>** comes *marriage;* procreation becomes an enduring bond between parents and children, namely *upbringing,* this being the free communication of one's own human essence in accordance with its ethical spiritual side, just as procreation is the natural communication of the same in accordance with the mere natural side. As such, in this spiritual ethical character, they are the *institution of the family* (p. 111).

The family is the central institution of society, "the center of human existence, the bond of individual life and common life, as it constitutes the complete satisfaction of the individual while also being the means by which the race, and thus the community, civil and religious, arises, both corporeally and ethically-spiritually (through upbringing)" (p. 114). Although a legal institution, it is (uniquely among legal institutions) primarily of a moral character, "in that according to its entire being it is the inner union and devotion of specific persons" (p. 113).

The cornerstone of the family is, of course, marriage. Here the complementarity of sexes comes to the foreground, in which this natural phenomenon becomes elevated into the realm of the personal: "from the mere union of sexual functions it is elevated into the union of persons for which the former only serves as substrate, thus into a bond not of mere momentary complementarity but of the persons concerned immutably becoming as one in feeling, knowledge, and will, into a *living union*" (p. 118). Its indispensable prerequisite is consent, but its form and structure are entirely independent thereof. And although it is primarily an ethical and secular relation, serving earthly society, its essence as pure devotion lends it a religious dimension which cannot be ignored. It therefore requires the blessing of God as bestowed by the church.

Restrictions on marriage involve near relation. The primary reason for this lies in the fundamental difference between the marriage bond and the bond between relations, especially **<xxiv>** between parents and children and between siblings. The marriage bond is a bond of mutual need, "a bond of necessitous, fulfillment-seeking, yearning love" (p. 135). The bond between parents and children, by contrast, is a bond of selfless love downward and reverence upward, while that between siblings is one without need, with "the organic purpose of *being* the family, of realizing its goal, not of *generating* the family, of being a means for it" (p. 135). These bonds cannot be confused or mingled. Furthermore, it serves the greater purpose of the human race for families not to close off to each other but rather to intermarry and so, in Augustine's words, to expand the bond of love.

Marriage is in principle indissoluble. There is only one true ground for dissolving a marriage, and that is adultery. In this day and age, civil government may extend the grounds of adultery by analogy to this ground, thus granting divorce on the basis of serious fault; but the church must remain faithful to Jesus' statement as recorded in Matthew ch. 5. Modernism has invented an alternative ground for divorce, which it even has the temerity to regard as the ethically superior ground – the spouse's happiness in life. To elevate such a principle to the grounds for divorce is to elevate personal satisfaction above the higher ethical order. It spells the destruction of ethical order.

Regarding religiously mixed marriages, marriages between persons of different religions are, for Christians, sinful unless concluded prior to conversion; but for persons of different Christian confessions, they are not per se sinful although in most cases they are to be discouraged. This can cause problems especially regarding the upbringing of children.

Paternal power is the power of parents over their children, not as an end in itself but with the goal of bringing them up to a state of civil and financial independence. (Stahl speaks **<xxv>** of paternal power, but he does so representationally; the discussion makes clear that both parents participate in this power.) It includes protection and representation vis-à-vis the outside world, and the power of upbringing, to determine what kind of education the children receive. Following independence, paternal power per se disappears, but the bonds of paternal love and filial piety remain.

The power of upbringing means that parents have the right and duty to determine the education of their children. But the state likewise has a "vocation and right" in this area. Broadly speaking, the paternal power extends to individual upbringing, state power to that which is involved in "national education," involving mores and culture, in particular with regard to training for public office. Furthermore, the state has the duty to ensure that schools meet minimum standards of quality. For its part, the church has the right to insist that nothing in the schools is taught contrary to the Christian faith.

Inheritance is the means by which personality extends itself through the generations. It therefore is not a mere transfer of property but a transfer of the entire sphere of rights and obligations from one generation to another. By means of inheritance, the human race maintains its coherence, by maintaining the separate legal spheres of its members integrally through the generations. The original form of succession is intestate, and it remains the model, even where testate succession is implemented. For intestate succession assumes that surviving spouses and children have the most right to the inheritance. Originally the male line was preferred in succession; but with the rise of Christianity the equality of the sexes has been increasingly realized in this regard as well, although with certain necessary exceptions (e.g., where landed property is connected with political position). **<xxvi>**

Stahl includes in an appendix a brief discussion of the value of Roman law. This discussion concisely reveals both the greatness and the shortcoming of that law. Firstly, Roman law was the first to realize the idea of law, without admixture either of morality or politics; secondly, it realized the principle of individual entitlement in a thorough, uncompromising fashion. But it failed to recognize other important principles, such as the connection between rights and duties, which led it to lopsided oddities, as Stahl details. But besides this, Roman law was able to implement a systematization of the law which remains exemplary for all time: that which Stahl characterizes as a codex of the nature of the case. For Roman law was more than a mere example of logical consistency; in terms of content as well, its system provides universally valid material, not certainly in terms of the law-ideas themselves, which is where the Romans fell short, but in terms of the nature of the case. "Should one consider that value [of Roman law] to lie in logical consistency, systematic completion, antique simplicity, that which is commonly understood as the scientific exemplariness of Roman law, thus only the *formal* aspect of the method of treatment, one thereby fails to appreciate that Roman law also contains a plethora of outstanding *material* decisions just as true for our conditions as for Roman" (p. 197).

PRIVATE LAW

INTRODUCTION

§. 1. The Principle of Personality in Law

<1> Private law comprises the relations in which the life of individual persons is fulfilled: *protection of the person* and his free action; *property**; *family*.

The principle through which the series of these relations appears as a unity, as a system, therefore is *the concept of man itself:* as ***personality,** built up from the* ***natural*** *creation and based on the natural creation.*

Accordingly, relations on the one hand develop subject to the conditions of natural, more specifically material, existence in accordance with their inherent *providentially administered goal* (τέλος): integrity of existence – maintenance and satisfaction through things – connection of generations and procreation.

On the other hand, however, these relations are elevated into the *essence of personality:* natural (material) existence is transformed into existence as a person, from which *freedom, honor, legal capacity,* etc.; natural satisfaction through things becomes material for the free manifestation of personality through the ordering of his lifestyle – from which *property;* and to this end persons may freely, by the power of immutable personal will, choose mutually to obligate themselves in an enduring fashion – through *contract.* The natural union of the sexes is elevated into that which is personal – into *marriage;* procreation, into upbringing *(paternal power)* and enduring bonds of piety, and <2> finally, through the extension of property beyond the grave to descendants, into *inheritance.*

Private law therefore springs from a dual principle: *the objective purpose* (τέλος) *of life relations* as grounded in the arrangement of nature (deeper: in the free divine providential administration); and the eternal *idea of personality* which, on the basis of the former, in the final analysis gives legal institutions their shape; both principles however in indissoluble permeation and unity.

The Kantian concept of "sensate, reasonable existence" would thus actually be the principle of private law if it were properly conceived. To wit, the "*sensate*" is not simply (subjectively) to be related to the nature of men but (objectively) to the economy of nature. Thus, legal relations (things, acts of others) are not as with Kant dead matter, idea-less objects, simply to be subsumed under an otherworldly abstract legal concept; on the contrary, precisely the aspect of legal formation lies within them, and not merely in the rationality of the person. Instead, then, of "the rational essence" we would more properly say "person," from which not only freedom would follow, as Kant and even more so Fichte one-sidedly and arbitrarily assume, but all those qualities belonging to the broad compass of the concept of personality as well, such as for example customary behavior [Sitte], steadfastness and so forth. These principles are just as much original elements of legal formation as is freedom.

PART ONE: THE RIGHT OF THE PERSON

Chapter 1: The Right of the Person in General

§. 2. The Rights of Personality

<3> Being a person, man is an original, independent and thus absolute end of creation and the world-plan (Book I [*Philosophical Foundations*], §. 6): not mankind as a genus, not the concept of man, but the individual, each individual person. The law must also conceive him as such. The individual person is consequently an absolute end in the legal order – this is the *right of the person* or the "*innate right*," the "*primeval right*." The content of this right therefore comprises the things belonging to the *existence of the person: integrity, freedom, honor, legal capacity, protection in acquired rights*. Individually these rights are viewed as "innate," though more properly they are viewed as rights inhering in the essence of personality.

The final ground of the right of the person is his being the *image of God*. This is also the case in his fallen condition, albeit in muddled, disturbed fashion. It is simply his essence, his concept. Therefore, his life must be held to be holy, room for his freedom and activity preserved, his value recognized.

Personality is the substrate of free action, not its allotted object, for which reason these fundamental rights are neither alienable nor disposable. From this follows the criminality of murder by another at one's own behest, the impermissibility of <4> Germanic feud law and dueling, contractual slavery, alienation of general legal capacity.

The *maxim of coexistence* is valid for these rights, and only for these rights, because they belong to each person independently in himself, and are not derived from a common higher organic relation, although even here this maxim is insufficient to ground a decision in the case of conflict; such can only be found in the specific nature of the rights concerned, as shown below (§§. 3 and 5).

It is as impossible as it is senseless individually to add up the objects and actions included in these rights of personality (such as for example the right to "speech instruments," to the use of members, such as "of the nose to smell," the right to make bodily movements, to dance, to wash oneself), should one desire to make an exhaustive list. Integrity and freedom include them all. Law, however, the concept of which after all is ethical power over others, only concerns the hindrance of others; my own use is not grounded in my right, but in my natural freedom, because God has given me a body (Book II [*Principles of Law*], §. 32). The exclusion of public restrictions, as for example that the state can make no laws regarding free passage or freedom of the press because such would infringe my right to free movement or the use of my speech instruments, therefore cannot be derived from the right of the person: natural freedom of the person must subordinate itself to the higher claims of common existence.

Because the right of the person is due men prior to any civil order as a primeval divine conferment, the atrophy of it in the civil order takes on the appearance of injustice (Book II [*Principles of Law*], §. 7), whereas the malign arrangement <5> of most of the other spheres largely seems only to be transgression of mores or inappropriateness.[9]

§. 3. The Right of the Person: Integrity

Integrity consists in the protection of life and limb, corporal inviolability, "peace" in the Germanic manner of speaking. It is the initial claim on the legal condition, thus preceding all others; in particular, it is the initial restriction on freedom. One's freedom should not infringe another's integrity.

§. 4. The Right of the Person: Freedom

Freedom is the power to act, that is, to be a cause in the external world according to one's own will and choice, to affect a *factual* situation (both to change one's spatial relation to actual situations, what the English call "vis loco motiva," and

---

[9] Hegel leaves no specific place at all for the rights of the person but rather confuses them with real rights [Sachenrechte] and considers them, to the degree that he gives them any attention at all, under the category of property. "As a person I have both my life and body, *like other things*, only to the degree that it is my will" (*Philosophy of Law*, §. 47). Therefore, I can *sell* my life, my members, my spatial freedom as well? The total divergence in meaning in which in the former case personality purely as such is the goal while in the latter case it is material satisfaction, as well as in the consequences, that in the latter case full disposability and alienability holds while in the former case it is ruled out, offers him no obstacle. The abstraction: "a thing is that which is entirely external to freedom, to which my life and body also belong," seems to him a sufficient ground for this confusion.

to act upon corporeal things and persons), and thus especially to affect *legal* situations.

It is part of the essence of personality that action is inseparable from its cause and becomes a component of the actor's existence. Therefore man expands his legal situation <6> through an act, his act (just as his personal existence itself) becoming binding on others; and he restricts it through an act, his act becoming binding on himself (for example occupation, dereliction, entering into inheritance, damage and so forth). What sort of act it must be, and what sort of legal consequences it has, are of course determined by the legal institutions in which it intervenes.

Because freedom arises from the law as an ethical order, it is not unrestricted but from the start has a specific content, standard and boundaries.

Legal freedom is bounded *first* by *higher duties* to which persons must subordinate themselves; not, of course, by claims of (subjective) morality, but indeed by ethical ideas of life relations maintained in common life (objective) – namely the ethical form of marriage, the state, the church and so forth; these are the one principle of the legal order, human freedom is the other. The kind and degree of this restriction can therefore only be determined by the nature of the legal institution concerned.

Freedom *furthermore* is restricted by the *equal freedom of others* (the maxim of coexistence). All legal objects are open to all. The conflicts that follow from this are not decided according to the consideration that these objects are to be distributed equally among all (the principle of equity: Book II [*Principles of Law*], §. 50), but, as is made clear above, simply according to the right of the person, his essence being *causality*. Therefore, the *act* is decisive. This is the preference of *priority* [Prävention], which comes into play whenever considerations grounded higher in the purpose of legal institutions are lacking. Others must take a back seat to those first making actual use of their freedom, who in taking possession of objects have put themselves in a favorable position. This priority is expressed differently according to the nature of relations, whether priority in a factual situation (place- <7> ment of nets in a stream, taking one's place in the theater), in the acquisition of a right (occupation), or in the grounding of a legal function (competence of the court).

§. 5. The Right of the Person: Honor

Honor is the consciousness people have of their *absolute value as a person.* Initially it is something internal. Others can do nothing to give or take away one's true honor. It is however a person's right to see this, his absolute value recognized by everyone in *common* life – this is *legal honor.*

The *basis* of honor, however, is above all *ethical integrity* as the true essence of a person, and therefore, especially with regard to the common life and thus legal honor, it is the public conviction of this integrity – *blamelessness* (**existimatio**). Honor therefore entails a double right, the right to it directly and the right to its basis. The former is *honor in the strict sense,* the latter is a *good reputation.*

There are therefore two forms of insulting a person's honor, underlain by various considerations. The former is infringed by acts directly demonstrating another's *contempt* (refusal to recognize honor) – *slander* (**injuria**); the latter through expressions that undeservedly deny one public recognition of blamelessness – *libel* and *calumny* (**diffamatio** and **calumnia**). Slander is unthinkable without *premeditation* to show contempt (**animus injuriandi**); this is not the case with the injury to the good name of another; on the other hand, libel is not unlawful if it is *true* (**exceptio veritatis**), while slander as such is by no means justified by the truth of the accusation. Slander and defamation [Diffamation] therefore are entirely different things, although they may vie in one and the same act. This essentially likewise **<8>** gives the sense of Roman law.[10] Against this, newer legislation often runs slander and calumny into each other.[11]

§. 6. The Right of the Person: Legal Capacity, Protection of Acquired Rights

Legal capacity in general is the characteristic of being the subject of rights – including the three mentioned general ones – and in this sense is the same thing as legal personality. In particular, however, it is the possibility of having specific rights (Book II [*Principles of Law*], §. 36), that is, the right to a certain object or a certain status as provided in the legal order in terms of its various subject areas.

Protection of acquired rights is maintenance in just these objects and statuses, the holding of which as a right is the concept of legal capacity, in particular in

---

[10]Walter in *Archiv für das Kriminalrecht* Vol. IV, p. 278.

[11]e.g., *Cod. Max. Bavar.* P. 4 cap. 17.

objects and statuses that can be gained or lost as an external possession, such as for example property or aristocratic privileges, rather than the ones that, once established, are immediately inseparable from the particular person to which they adhere (such as paternal authority and the marriage bond).

§. 7. Slavery

The complete lack of recognition of these rights located in the essence of the person is *slavery*, as it was found in ancient states, as it also still exists among contemporary Asian peoples, but also as it is found even in the southern states of the Union of North America. **<9>**

Slavery consists in the treatment of men not as a person, not as an end in himself, but as a thing, as a mere means for others. It is therefore to be rejected out of hand. It is no justification that some men are incapable by nature of caring for themselves (Aristotle), for this leads only to the conclusion that they need to be put under the guidance and power of another, not however that they be made into mere means for that other. There is no justification for it in the rationale that otherwise prisoners of war will be killed (Hugo), for it is precisely this killing that is to be rejected. Even if there are laws that effectively protect slaves from murder, mutilation, destruction by punishment, exhaustion through labor, the separation of families (spouses from each other, children from parents) through sale or disposal by the owners, the sale of a man as such, the position as a whole of being a mere implement of labor and object of use for another and to be entirely at another's disposal, one's own lack of legal capacity, which furthermore renders inoperative those protective laws – these things taken individually and as a whole unconditionally constitute the destruction of the right of the person, a disparagement of the image of God, a violation of the commandments of God in the hindering of slaves in their observance of those commandments.

Now then, where slavery exists and as long as it exists it is, as is all positive law, lawful and binding. It could certainly have the appearance that the slave, for whom the social order preserves no right but confronts him merely as something oppressive, would also have no duty of obedience against it, and that resistance, insurgence, any form of self-defense, would be allowed to him. Nevertheless, ethics preserves, even in ever so slight degree, that which the law denies, and the order which curtails him is still always an order and therefore also an order <10> for him. Therefore, the Christian commandment says: you slaves, obey your masters in the flesh!

Transition phases, similar for example to German serfdom, to maintain order, the protection of the ruling class or for the entire economic condition of the total population may be necessary and therefore justified. But there is no justification for maintaining the condition of slavery itself, even if only for a period of time.

Germanic *serfdom* is not an annihilation of personality in the way slavery is. The serf is the subject of laws, is not a thing, is only subject to conscription in his person, is not an object of property. But the serf nevertheless lacks essential rights of the person, such as the free choice of occupation, the freedom of domicile. Serfdom had therefore also to give way, as is recognized, and that the serf often had it better than the contemporary free proletarian could and should not have halted a development based in an ethical postulate, the fundamental recognition of the right of the person.

§. 8. The Right of the Person: Inalienable Freedom

The thought of the absolute claim that the person qua person has rights and is to be protected in those rights was lacking in the earlier epoch of natural law; hence, even the condition of slavery (for example von Oldendorp, Grotius, Thomasius, Wolff, Höpfner)[12] was considered permissible. First Rousseau and then Kant made inalienable freedom an absolute right of the person – as Kant put it: "a man must not be made into a bare means!" However aside from the fact that Rousseau et al. conceived this right only negatively and therefore without <11> content,[13] while ruling out protection in acquired rights, they founded the entire objective legal structure one-sidedly on the rights of man. Against this, Hegel, as already mentioned, restored the legal status of ethical institutions, the family and the state; but to do this he in fact gave away the *right of the person* through his pantheistic standpoint, substituting for it simply the bare concept (aspect) of personality or subjectivity. According to him, the *individual* person is simply "an accident of general being"[14]; this aspect of subjectivity rather than the individual particular person is for him the goal of creation and therefore also of law.

---

[12]See Vol. I (2nd ed.), p. 155 [*The Rise and Fall of Natural Law,* pp. 133–134].

[13]*Ibid.*, p. 150 [*The Rise and Fall of Natural Law,* pp. 128ff.].

[14]Hegel, *Philosophy of Law*, p. 145.

Chapter 2: Freedom and Equality

§. 9. Moral Freedom

<13> *Freedom,* being an inseparable attribute of personality, is a primeval right of man. Its circumference is discerned from its proper understanding:

The essence of freedom is *to be determined only by one's own self.* Inner, moral freedom, therefore, is to be determined only by one's own self in one's own resolutions, while outward, legal freedom is to be determined only by one's own self in one's actions in human community. The former is freedom of the will in the strict sense, the latter freedom of action.

The innermost self of man is however a *determinate ethical essence;* it is *consciousness* of the same and the decisive exclusion of what is opposed to it; it is *individuality,* and so unending creative choice as the manifestation of individuality (Book I [*Philosophical Foundations*], §. 39). Inner, moral freedom thus does not exist where man cannot act according to his ethical essence and in consciousness of that essence, and according to his individuality. Man, determined by sin and the passions, submitting to the flesh rather than to the spirit, is not free, but unfree; because sin and the passions are not the self of man, but a power standing in opposition to his essence. A child who obeys before having full cognizance of commands is at the least less free. But man is still not free when in religion he stands under the law, in morality under the maxim, in art under a style, instead of under grace, love, creative conviction; for although law, maxims, <14> rules do not stand in opposition to his ethical essence, they do restrict his individuality.

Therefore *choice* certainly forms part of moral freedom. Moral freedom means not being bound to an exhaustive blueprint that in itself and thus completely, positively determines our actions, that subordinates man only to that which all men have as a common equal essence, which leaves no room to individuality which is ours and which is originally productive. Man is not free when, in fulfilling his duties as son, father, relative, citizen, he does so not by being original and special but rather by thoughtless imitation. Even so, the release from strictures, this choice, must always be based on necessity and constraint. Choice in terms of the good, not the choice between good and evil, pertains to ethical freedom. The choice between good and evil which actually confronts man is a consequence of a division of his being, the consequence of being ruled, tempted, by a power alien to his essence – evil – and is not freedom but disturbance; it is an attack on his freedom. The more perfect the character, the higher the level of freedom; the less of a choice between good and evil, the less possibility of evil, ignoble, dishonorable decisions. Will the man who considers whether or not to steal, to lie, who being a soldier at his post, considers whether to abandon it, be considered freer, or the one for whom there is no possibility of stealing, of lying, of fleeing his duty, who can act only according to conscience and honor? It is not the vacillating character, still in a position to choose between good and evil, which is free, but the steadfast character that has become a law of unavoidable nature and necessity (Book I [*Philosophical Foundations*], §. 40).

In God, the highest personality, the aspects of freedom are present absolutely: an absolute immutable essence, which is God's holiness and wisdom – the absolute conscious exclusion of everything ungodly, unholy – absolute boundless, immea- **<15>** surable individuality and creative power, all in complete harmony. Human freedom on the other hand needs to advance and is called to advance in all its aspects, and considering that the essence of man is permeated with sin, it is divided and in contradiction in all its aspects. Man is to advance by gaining in consciousness and in decisiveness in excluding that which is contrary to his essence, which is evil. Therefore, the one who through reflection has succeeded in gaining this advancement occupies a higher level and is freer than the naive and childlike man; the attainment of this decidedness is the reason God allowed and allows temptation. At the same time man is to advance to a greater expression and freer revelation of individuality; he is called to greater creativity. But while the essence of man is not divine and holy but is capable of providing a basis for an existence separated from God, a basis for self-seeking – for this reason the consciousness of the contradictions in his ethical essence became a temptation to him and brought him to a fall; and after having fallen, the free revelation of his individuality also became a burgeoning revelation of this sin and the advance and confirmation of the same. Therefore, a conflict arises among the relations of human freedom, with the preservation of man's ethical essence threatened by the advance of consciousness and individuality. The advance of consciousness threatens innocence and purity, and the advance of individuality (in the particular sense of Christian freedom) threatens the strictness of laws and adherence to duty. The leading of the human race and the moral development of each individual moves through these hurdles.

§. 10. Legal Freedom and Freedom of Choice

Outward, legal freedom concerns external actions in social life, determined not by other persons, in particular the ar- **<16>** bitrary will of the ruling authority, but by one's self. It therefore is characterized by these elements: that this order to which we are subordinated be in accordance with our true inner self, which is the truly ethical, reasonable life-order; that insight into its laws and its foundations be accessible to us so that we consciously can obey it; that it provide our individuality with all the room it needs. We are not free in the legal sense when we are put under immoral [unsittlichen], unreasonable laws, or where law remains a secret of a certain class, or where otherwise reasonable laws through obsolescence cease to allow room for our individuality, either by suppressing our national individuality or by restricting our personal individuality. Finally, we are totally unfree in the legal sense where a tyrannical government simultaneously suppresses that order which accords with our ethical essence and our individuality as well.

The first condition of legal freedom is thus the reasonableness of laws. The unreasonableness and thus immorality of laws is the first suppression of freedom. By contrast, the maintenance of a public life-order in the people and this order's restriction of our actions is not in itself a reduction of our freedom but rather a postulate of it. When this order truly is ethically reasonable, it sets us not against our actual self but in accordance with it. When we are required by the legal order not to divorce arbitrarily, to obey our elders, to provide for and educate our children, etc., all of this is only the condition of our true inner self. And vice versa, if a legal order loses sight of all of this, we have not gained any greater freedom, because we dare not make any use of such latitude; we are left with only the support of our own ethical essence for our actions and have thus lost a support of our freedom. This leads to the collapse of mores among the great mass, uncertain of its own ethical essence, as well as in the upcoming generation; thus we have gained unfreedom. **<17>**

But there is more! The ethical life-order of the people is likewise the general validity of our own ethical essence in the external world, and therefore the highest guarantee of our freedom. This is because that which is in the highest degree my freedom is realized when my ethical essence and fiber, thus my inner self, my true will striving for realization and dominion, finds expression not simply in my own actions but also in the condition of the nation, and it is a violation of my freedom when contrary actions remove the prospect and impression of an ethically ordered common life – removes what we might call the ethical atmosphere – when I must tolerate what violates my ethical or religious sensibility – when public institutions neglect what this sensibility requires. Therefore the freedom of each entails the right to the existence of such a life-order in which the family is maintained in its ethical shape, the church in its purity of faith, the entirety of public life in discipline and honor and unto the glory of God. It is not a violation of freedom to forbid and punish public disrespect, blasphemy, convenience divorce, but rather its establishment; it is not the maintenance of church confessions, church discipline, Sunday observance but rather their abandonment, not church marriage but civil marriage which violates freedom.[15]

No less a demand of freedom, however, is the full expression of our individuality. The maintenance of this kind of ethically reasonable life-order among the people should not go so far as to cut this off. Partly it must not encroach upon the sphere to which our innermost personality or the creative use of our God-given gifts belongs; partly it must progressively leave more and more room to individual decision in such areas as choice of occupation, choice of spouse, choice of faith, free scientific research and dissemination, free political endeavor. **<18>**

Therefore choice is also an indispensable element of legal freedom, in fact it is the blossoming of freedom, because choice is the expression of individuality. Even so, in legal freedom as well this choice must have a basis in ethical necessity. Just as the ethical essence of man forms the basis for inner ethical freedom, the ethical life-order of a people forms the basis for external legal freedom.

The ethical life-order of the people and the free manifestation of individuality by individual persons permeate each other without a specific dividing line, with the result that with the latter a conflict arises for external freedom (as it does in the former case with internal freedom), that the strictness of the ethical life-order of the people – especially while it is in the hand of human and thus imperfect magistrates – might prejudice true ethical individuality, and vice versa: the full development of individuality might prejudice the ethical life-

---

[15]Stahl, *Seventeen Parliamentary Speeches*, p. 61.

order. Therefore, true legal freedom must rest on both bases, with the point being to bring them into harmony in the most appropriate way and in accordance with circumstances.

Calvin's order in Geneva preserved a high degree of freedom for the believing congregation, because it expressed and put into practice to a high degree its innermost self, a truly religious, and more to the point a specific religious conviction; tolerance of libertinism lost its freedom. Considered in itself, however, this order restricted the expression of individuality, the more so as it was not lacking in a heavy admixture of human one-sidedness and narrowness, and thus did not entirely answer to the general human essence. On the other hand, to drop ethics from legislation as occurred at the end of the 18th century is the other extreme; this is not freedom but the abolition of freedom. **<19>**

§. 11. Freedom versus License

These considerations lead to the following fundamental theses:

Legal freedom is bounded by the equal freedom of others: the maxim of co-existence.

Legal freedom is originally and in itself bounded, or better, determined by the ethical life-order of a people, and thus by the law of life-relations (family, community, station, church, etc.), differently according to each.

No right to unrestricted freedom can obtain in any area. Thus for example there is no right to unrestricted establishment of sects, no right to the unrestricted use of the labor forces in the society (Turgot). The public order of religion or of production for gain require limits and these themselves then form a postulate of true freedom.

There can be no right to that which is bad and repulsive in itself and unconditionally, for example to an atheistic religious confession and the education of children in the same, to an immoral lifestyle, total profligacy, and the like.

It is not society's responsibility to increase the choice between good and evil, so as to make men freer. Such a choice is not freedom, and its increase is not progress. To lead into temptation for the sake of resoluteness is a matter for God alone because He also provides the strength to triumph over the temptation; it is not a matter for human government and leading (Book I [*Philosophical Foundations*], §. 40).

By contrast, the task is to augment individuality and the possibilities for its manifestation. This is true freedom and thus true progress. By extension this requires the tempering or abolition of preventive measures such as censorship, denial of freedom of association, and enhancement of the freedom to choose a calling since no class is any longer restricted from any <20> vocation. But this augmentation of individuality and its free manifestation can in no way serve as the basis for a freedom that undermines ethical public order and the meaning behind that order. Thus for example when a people preserves its religious ethical substance, as did, it must be recognized, the English people in the 16th and 17th centuries despite the plethora of errors, it also had a right to freedom of the press, which was useful to it and constituted a true elevation of its freedom. When however a people has abandoned that religious ethical substance, like the French at the end of the 18th century, then there can be no right to freedom of the press; in fact the latter becomes an affront to justice and does not elevate its freedom but rather helps to destroy the people's ethical goods and thus also that portion of freedom which it still had.

§. 12. The Modern Concept of Freedom

The fundamental error in this age's claim to freedom lies in the fact that it sees freedom as an empty formal possibility without content or goal, without a determinate ethical essence. Accordingly, a person appears to be morally the freer the greater the choice he has between good and evil, the more his consciousness becomes a tabula rasa, until finally reaching the zero point, a person bound and determined by nothing decides whether to be the most repulsive cad or the most elevated wise man. Thus legally a person appears the freer the more the public order allows all thinkable, including the most repulsive, options to be displayed before him: God-denying confession, an unrestrained press, riotous unions, frivolous carousals, the pursuit of gain which destroys the common welfare.

Rousseau's train of thought rests on just this error. He also detaches the freedom of men fully from the ethical substance of men, which is their true concept. Rousseau was en- <21> tirely correct, that freedom is inalienable and hence could not be alienated by participating in the state, nor could it be alienated to the state, and he was entirely justified in thinking that for this reason the problem of the state relation is this, that every man, in that he obeys the state power, only obey himself and therefore remain as free as before ("chacun s'unissant à tous, n'obeisse pourtant qu'à lui-même et reste aussi libre qu'auparavant" [*Du Contrat Social,* I. 6]). But since he formally conceived of freedom as unrestrictedness, as arbitrariness, he arrives, as elaborated elsewhere (Book I [*Philosophical Foundations*], §. 50), at a solution to the problem in the *formal* criterion of how the laws come to exist, in the equal competition of all in the state power, by which indeed freedom does not remain unalienated, but becomes completely alienated to the majority. In truth, however, freedom is not separable from the ethical essence of men, and on this basis the solution to this problem lies only in the *material* aspect, in the content of the laws and the government, that they only command what my own ethical essence and my own rational life-purpose requires. For in this case and only in this case do I, in that I obey the ruling authority, obey only myself (that which is my true self) and hence remain as free as before. That this solution, given the shortcoming of the earthly condition, only imperfectly and approximately can be achieved, is self-evident. One must accept this just as one must accept mortality and imperfect health. The false conception likewise obstructs the solution as much as possible, however, leading to a situation where the formal participation of all is accompanied by content that is virtually contrary to the claims of ethics and human reason, for which reason everyone becomes oppressed as never before. **<22>**

§. 13. Equality

Equality is a primeval right of man, albeit in specific measure, according to a specific relation. It does not rule out distinctions and rank, the inequality of actual rights, the inequality even of the capacity for rights. Abstract and unconditional equality ("égalité") is by no means a primeval right of man.

In fact, the essence of man as person requires the equality of right: that to which one can lay claim because he is a person (image of God) must also be claimable by the other. But the plan of the ethical world requires inequality of rights. Because this plan gives people differing positions and tasks, they must also have different rights. As a person, man is an absolute totality for himself; this is the basis for equality of rights. However, man is also a part and member of organic connections and institutions, and no organism is composed of equal members; this is the basis for inequality of rights.

The considerations decisive to inequality are the diversity of natural characteristics, the diversity of vocation, the diversity of prior acts, and destiny.

Inequality of rights is grounded above all in the *natural diversity* of people: sex, age, health, even education. Inequality upon this basis is still seldom disputed even though examples are not lacking of philosophers, consistently carrying out the concept of equality, declaring the exclusion of women from public offices and legislative bodies to be a violation of human rights. Even rights that otherwise must be generally accorded can be denied due to natural hindrances such as insanity.

Inequality of rights is further grounded in the *diversity of vocations* and the characteristics, both natural and civil, which relate to those vocations. The law [Das Gesetz] of the relevant relations provides each the measure of his rights according to <23> his position in those relations. This is the case with the family; husband, wife, and children each with their own task and their own rights – this is disputed by no one. This is no less the case, however, with state and church. Inequality in the state is not simply connected to the diversity of intellectual gifts, something which even the French Revolution recognized, but to the difference of every other quality decisive to the proper ordering of the public condition. The essential character of the state, rather than the right of personality, is decisive to the question whether this inequality consists in a simple function or an enduring right, whether it is personal or hereditary. So for example it is part of the essential character of the state whether participation in its confession of faith is required for participation in its administration; whether a material interest in land, especially landholding, is required to take up a position in the representative body, princely birth to inherit the crown, etc. Just as people are not mere means for the state, the state is not a mere means for the people: participation in its administration must not be motivated by honor, income, enjoyment of ruling, etc., or by the sense of equality as such. Accordingly, inequality on this basis is then to be related to political rights per se, not to private law and not to class-based occupations and branches of industry, except where these are inseparably associated with political institutions. And they must not extend beyond the limits of the vocation. An inequality of rights, thus a privilege, which is not grounded in any vocation, is a **privilegium**; this is an unfair relation, or where it is grounded in historical occurrences and thus justified, nevertheless a relation to be restricted to the strictly necessary. So for example it is no **privilegium** that a large landholder has a dominant share in a country's representative body, but it is a **privilegium** when he is exempt from quartering soldiers or mortgage duties or when his sons have exclusive capacity for state offices. To eliminate privileges is <24> natural progress, to eliminate rights of station [Standesrechte] is a disturbance contrary to nature.

Finally, inequality of rights is grounded in the *dissimilarity of preceding acts and occurrences* and the rights acquired through them. When someone gets a wife and raises a son, he has a family-right over them that a bachelor does not have. It is the same when property is acquired or inherited. It is the same when a class, a city, a family has acquired political rights in the previous history of the country (more over this in the following chapter).

§. 14. Essential Equality, Accidental Inequality

All these inequalities must however preserve as their basis the essential equality of rights residing in the essence of the person. This is the truth in the error of the Revolution. There is a general civil right and honor which must be the substance of the legal condition. Inequalities must only be accidental to this, just as personality and its essence is the substance of man and the variety of vocations only the accident. So for example where in their previous position the Jews, and indeed often Christian confessions, were not allowed religious exercise, human existence atrophied. This essential equality was contradicted by gradations in penal law, where violations against nobles were punished more strictly than violations against civilians, or where one class was subject to corporal punishment and the other not. Thus it is a proper progression in equality that civilians can attain to manors and attendant positions in the representative body, that public offices in civil and military service be open to all. In the area of ethics such an essential equality should also exist; this is an advance of the times; nevertheless, differences ought not cease to exist: the elderly are entitled to a different sort of honor than the young; <25> the upper classes, the ruling authority are entitled to a different sort of honor. The task of this age does not lie in the elimination of distinctions, the leveling of political conditions, as the Revolution would have it, but in the *recovery of essential equality in the maintenance of grounded distinctions*. As in the Middle Ages knightly honor and law formed the common substance (albeit for a restricted circle) in the light of which distinctions were less significant, and regardless of superiority and inferiority, regardless of the deep subjection to the power of kingship, even the humblest knight was considered the equal of the king – this is Burke's impassioned description – so in our time (for society as a whole) function human right and human worth.

Equality before the law is a truth and an advance of the times when understood as this essential citizenship common to all; it is an error and worthless notion when it is made to mean the abolition of legal distinctions, especially distinctions of station.

The false concept of equality is the major force of destruction since the end of the last century. It entails unconditionally the impermissibility of kingship, of state religion, of political rights of landholders, and everything of this sort, it entails the abolition of the organic edifice of the state.[16] The most foolish effort along these lines had to be the enterprise of carrying through this equality not simply in the area of law but also in the area of mores, to achieve through laws or moral coercion the fully equal treatment of the "citizen general" and the "citizen barbarian."

[16]Kant, *Doctrine of Law* XLV, understands this equality only formally, not to obligate oneself to another in greater degree than one *can* bind another to oneself; this is of course theoretically erroneous, in that society does not rest on mutually engaged commitments, but is practically without consequence, in that it admits true inequality when only the mere possibility of the highest entitlement for everyone remains conceivable.

Chapter 3: Protection of Acquired Rights

§. 15. Acquired Rights as the Expression of Personality

<27> Protection of acquired rights is an original right of man.

Acquired rights, as the name itself suggests, are not coeval with the existence of the person but presuppose certain actions or certain occurrences and conditions, and thus do not form part of the rights of personality. What does form part of the rights of personality is the inviolable maintenance of acquired rights *after* they have been acquired. The rights acquired by individuals stand in opposition to innate rights, but the protection in acquired rights is itself a natural right. The complete worth of man as a person is found only in this stability of all legally acquired rights. This is because it is part of the essence of the person to be active for his condition and to be certain of his condition. The person is an *acting* subject; if therefore man is a person, his *act* must be recognized, and thus the *rights that arise from his act.* A person's legal condition should not simply be the result of his *concept as personality;* it must also, to some degree, be his *own work* as well, the result of his *actions* and the actions of other persons. And because in the existing order these are appropriately (legally) grounded or have been gained through achievement, so they must remain inviolable as an expansion of his self, as his world, over which his will is established for the present and future. Otherwise he is not truly treated as a person but simply as a concept or object to which certain effects are due of neces- <28> sity. Thus the most masculine, powerful peoples hold acquired rights in the highest honor: the Romans, the Germans, and – in particular up until the present age – the English; and where this high honor does not exist, as with the Orientals and the Greeks, there it is that this whole depth and strength of personality is lacking. It is therefore a great error of the Revolution – and more or less the natural law theory – that in protecting, even imposing, what it derives from the concept of man it believes that it is upholding man and his rights, but yet refuses to recognize the result of his actions, *acquired rights*. It thus removes from him his self-causality and refuses him the certainty of his legal sphere; it preserves for him only what at any given moment others regard as his right, not what is his right in an unambiguous objective order. This is not the restoration but the destruction of the rights of man.[17]

Herein lies a broader ground for legal inequality beyond that contained in the organic nature of legal institutions, especially the state, as was already indicated in previous sections. In the private sphere, distinctions in wealth arise hereby, and it would mean the dissolution of society should one, as the Communists aim to do, wish not to recognize acquired rights but rather the equality of possessions, presumably in accordance with the nature of man. But political positions are also ac- **<29>** quired as rights in this manner, partly as the individual historical formation of an organic position grounded in the essence of the state (e.g. rights of the English peerage), partly however as truly accidental rights without any inner ground in the essence of the state. It should be said however that the legal situation is not perfect, nor even appropriate, in which these accidental political rights and inequalities can arise; nevertheless, once having arisen in a legal manner they must be held in regard and protected by virtue of the right of the person. This is especially true for so-called feudal rights. Their appropriateness to times past or present is irrelevant. One may dispute about that and come to a differing judgment for differing rights. Their legality in former times is beyond doubt, and since then they are equal to all other acquired rights. No time is called to hold court over the past and rights arisen in the past, and to recognize or abolish them in accordance with its verdict regarding their appropriateness.

---

[17]This error is most closely connected with the rationalistic principle: recognition only of that which follows logically, exclusion of everything the cause of which is personality, freedom, act (cf. Vol. I, p. 142 [*The Rise and Fall of Natural Law,* p. 119]). Hence Hegel as well, although asserting the organic coherence of the state over against the aggregational conception of liberalism, nevertheless had no sense of *acquired rights*. This is shown in his treatments concerning the Württemberg territorial estates and the English Reform Bill, but most blatantly in his *Philosophy of History* (p. 263), where he pictures the Roman respect for existing laws and acquired rights, in consequence of which e.g. "It took Licinius ten years to carry laws favorable to the plebs" and the like, with the greatest revulsion, characterizing them as a "disposition and character" the "foundational aspect" of which lies in "that primal *robber-community.*"

§. 16. Limits on Acquired Rights

Like all human freedom and action, acquired rights are bounded in their validity by that which the idea of the common condition and the legal order, or the natural continuing development of the same, promotes or excludes with unavoidable necessity. From this follows:

1. Acquired rights cannot be considered inviolable to the degree that they eliminate another's right of personality, e.g., the slave trader appeals in vain to his **jus quaesitum**. It is similar to the way the freedom of the one cannot be allowed to violate the integrity of another.

2. In developed state constitutions, in which each member has an organic position designated for the sake of the <30> whole, *for the future* essentially no acquisition of new political rights, no inequality, can take place through mere incidental actions of individual members.

3. In the overarching world-historical development of the public condition in its entirety, acquired rights of individual persons or classes in the final analysis must give way, because they are in constant relation to the entirety and only derive their protection from that entirety; they can be changed, even absorbed. However, even then they must, where the public well-being no longer can support them, give place *as rights* and be *recognized as such*, and in the most considerate manner, if at all possible with compensation. The violent abolition of acquired rights out of political considerations is not a progressive and regular function of the state organism but the work of extraordinary times, and therefore is better viewed as a world-historical than a juridical phenomenon.

§. 17. Rights versus the Common Good

The newer school culminating in the French Revolution does not recognize the concept of acquired rights; for it, rights arise at any moment, like new from top to bottom, through reason and the popular will. This is the view not only regarding specifically political rights (rights to rulership) but also regarding all rights of acquisition and property* as far as they are, or appear to be, involved with a political institution – for example, so-called feudal rights, toll and trade rights, immunities and the like. This school only recognizes the concept of acquired rights as regarding pure private property, which is a right which completely isolates the one against the other; and it does so inconsistently, because if the present is at all called to judge the past and to investigate the title of rights derived from the past, then this calling holds for all rights without distinc- **<31>** tion, and this great investigation must concern itself not only with the rationality of feudal rights but also with the rationality of property.

Since it does not go this far, the newer school (liberalism) does recognize acquired rights, justifying their abolition by way of exception, in terms of the undeniable admissibility of what is required to maintain the public condition. Even here, however, it far exceeds the true principle in manner and measure. It considers abolition to be justified for the common good (**salus publica**, bien publique), by which it understands not *public necessity*, which is the irrefutable need for healthy, salutary continuity and organic development, but rather *bare utility* (**lucrum**), and often by this utility intending the utility of the *majority*, thus the people over against the upper classes, rather than the well-being of the whole. There are however no legal grounds for removing the rights or possessions of individuals or minorities because *advantageous* to someone else, or the majority, or even the state. And then it is often a simply imaginary utility, a mere doctrinaire ideal for which acquired rights are violated, as for example with the so-called liberation of landed property. Furthermore, these rights are not yielded up as rights, as in the case of conflict between the development of the public condition and individual rights, with the latter considered inferior; it does not even recognize these individual rights where they are, or appear to be, an affront to the common existence; it wipes them out at once as something unlawful.

This entire approach led to the more or less inconsiderate and unjustified abolition of acquired rights, eventually to the radical destruction of the legal situation and the refusal of compensation. Taking the lead in Europe in this regard was the notorious night of August 4th 1789 ("the St. Bartholomew's Day of property"). The recognition of this fact cannot be denied out of consideration of the motive of personal sacrifice **<32>** for the public welfare, nor from the fact that multiple legal institutions (serfdom, incidental tribute and the like) needed to be abolished or changed. Apart from the degree to which terrorism, false sentimentality, womanizing vanity determined actions, this abolition of existing rights in individual cases was often entirely unfounded and even partly chimerical – e.g., the abolition of guilds, hunting laws, the inequality of imposts (?), fees for ecclesiastical services – and as a whole was carried out in such excess and upheaval of social conditions and gave such a shock to legal principles that it could not have been guided by true political or economic utility. The *Declaration of the Rights of Man* in the same year constituted the fulfillment of the announcements made that night, and by way of completion the matter was closed through the law of July 17th 1793, which abolished all feudal rights without compensation.

In Germany, such a radical implementation of these false principles did not take place because the Revolution did not there become fully realized. On the other hand, such was at least contemplated and announced in 1848, in the "basic rights" of the German national assembly, and was realized in at least a few acts, such as the abolition of all rights of previously entitled orders, the knighthood, the Prussian hunting law. Even after 1848, the oft unfounded abolition of rights was proclaimed either with insufficient compensation or none at all. The worst example of this was the intervention in the property rights of the church; the grossest irony is that this was viewed as taking place out of a supreme consideration for the public welfare (**salus publica suprema lex esto**) when in fact the majesty and security of the church's property was offered up to benefit individuals.[18] While all this forms part and parcel of a volatile <33> period, it continues to be the widespread opinion that every forced renunciation of acquired rights for the true or alleged improvement of the public condition is justified, especially where money compensation is offered. The most extreme and factually unrealizable exaggeration from the opposite end of the spectrum is that of the Haller school, which considers rights once they have arisen to be absolutely inviolable for all eternity. This makes the rights of man just as much an exclusive principle as does the liberal theory. It is the consequence of the private-law absolute isolation of rights.

§. 18. Expropriation of Property

Differing from the *abolition of rights*, which removes the recognition and operation of an entire genus of rights in the state, is the *expropriation* of things, which extorts from individuals individual objects of continuously recognized rights, namely property rights. The former is a legislative act and is based on the continuous development of the legal condition, the latter is an administrative act

---

[18] Stahl, *Speeches*, pp. 63ff., "The Liquidation of Church Revenues" [Die Ablösung der Kircheneinkünfte], and 70ff., "The Forced Liquidation of Assets" [die Zwangsablösung unter dem Werthe].

based on the continuous movement of material (industrial, commercial and the like) conditions. Therefore expropriation is a continuously exercised function of state power, while the abolition of rights is not. However, the principle behind both is the same: the *public necessity* as distinguished from mere *common utility*. This is of fundamental importance. In accordance with this, expropriation is appropriate for fortifications, dikes, roadways, railways, to build churches, schools, hospitals where this otherwise would not be possible or at least not in any useful way, in particular for the expansion of previously existing buildings. On the con- <34> trary, it is not appropriate to expropriate the house of a private individual because it would provide the most advantageous solution for a public establishment [Etablissement], nor to expropriate private land because it would be the most efficient for new construction sites and the like, and especially not for state buildings, because even without expropriation these can always be built through additional spending. Most of all, expropriation cannot be justified for mere *beautification*. Expropriation for *any "public goal"* is therefore a despicable maxim. The presumed advantage that it brings does not in the least offset the damage done to the security of property, because the security and strength of property and the attitude it fosters are certainly no less significant components of the common welfare than are enterprises of common utility.

Grotius, the first person scientifically to put forward the foundational statement of expropriation (**dominium eminens civitatis**),[19] ascribes appropriateness simply to *public utility* in opposition to *extreme need* (**summa necessitatis**). The latter he understands only as the so-called *right of necessity,* that is immediate, extreme physical need (for example, fire), which even empowers private individuals to infringe alien property (**quae privatis quoque jus aliquod in aliena concedit**). But the concept of public utility lacks necessary, strict boundaries. In this unrestricted manner, a point of view has taken control leading in the end to the excessive extension of expropriation, as witness recent legislation.[20] By contrast, the *Berlin Political Weekly* does not wish to restrict expropriation to the case of physical need, danger of flooding and fire, if the development of general trade requiring e.g. railways is not likewise an undeniable need to the country. <35> However, the principle of expropriation is not the right of necessity as

---

[19]Grotius, *De Jure Belli et Pacis,* Book III, ch. 20 §.7, likewise Book II, ch. 14 §. 7.

[20]e.g., the Baden legislation of August 28th 1835.

proposed by the *Political Weekly*, which knows no commandment, and which, as Grotius already indicated, also accrues to any private individual, as little as it is the advantage of the majority or of the state; but rather, the necessary organic development of the common condition and the necessary participation and thus shared involvement by individuals in it.

Chapter 4: The Principle of Humanity

§. 19. Universal Human Value

<37> The image of God in man is the final ground of the right of the person (§. 2). In it lies the obligation on the civil order not only to preserve the rights necessary merely for the existence of the person, but also to elevate him to an ever higher level of entitlement, freedom and gratification, which we described above as the primeval right (Book II [*Principles of Law*], §. 36). It is this power which motivates our times at their deepest level.

Among the many partly true, partly misconceived efforts of these times, one appears in full clarity: the *recognition of the rights of man*. This does not belong simply to the area of law. More deeply comprehended, it is the *principle of humanity:* the idea that the well-being, the right, the honor of every individual, even the most humble, is the concern of the community, which views each person in accordance with his individuality, which protects, honors, looks after him without regard for descent, class, race, gift, as long as he has a human face. This is the characteristic principle of the times and what constitutes its true worth. From it stems the abolition of serfdom, torture, the toleration of deviant religious confessions, the elevation of lower classes to equal civil honor, the many philanthropic pursuits, the effort to provide a satisfactory existence for the starving masses. This principle was alien to previous times, even that of the Reformation. Certainly, where Christian faith exists, love of neighbor and thus humanity is of necessity the motiva- <38> tion of life. However, this neighborly love in the past only concerned corporeal and spiritual well-being, not entitlement, freedom, the honor of men, and only provided the motivation for personal action, not the civil order. The outlook of improving entire classes out of a motivation of humanity, of spiritual individuality, of recognizing the honor of each person, did not inspire any institution in those times. Only in the most recent period has humanity in its full concept become an energetic virtue, the principle determining the entire society.

§. 20. The Fear of God as Principle of Order

On the other hand, earlier periods of European Christianity had the *fear of God* as the motivation for the public order, the unconditional devotion to God's command and ordinances and the zeal to glorify God. Recent times prior to the revival of Christian faith (that is, the end of the 18th and beginning of the 19th century), had eliminated this motivation. Every trace of the recognition of an unconditional divine command, every obligation to fulfill the will of the living God disappeared from it. Only the recognition of men and their convictions and opinions, and the care for men, remained as guideline. Thus in the area of religion only tolerance remained a recognized and praised motivation, not however the zeal for God's Word and God's honor, that previously was the only such recognized motivation. Tolerance has no boundaries; all religious or much rather irreligious doctrines are to have equal rights and equal honor; and even deistic and pantheistic doctrine of every stripe is to be recognized as Christian and as a church as long as it considers itself to be so. On the other hand, fidelity to divine truth, to maintain the true revelation of God, finds no consideration when it maintains its true measure, much less so when it in any way oversteps its boundaries. It is the same in the po- **<39>** litical arena. The state is based solely on human rights, not on higher goals; this is the sympathy for all opposition against all authority; it lacks the recognition of unconditional commands for the legal order. From this springs opposition to the death penalty and in fact to any sort of punishment. In the absence of a higher command that the criminal must be punished, that where blood is shed, blood must be shed, this becomes an institution for improving the criminal or a means of providing for the security for others. From this springs the claim for unconditional divorce, making the happiness of the spouses, their sense of what is agreeable, the decisive concern and not the higher, unconditional command that what God has joined together, let no man tear asunder. From this everywhere stems the revolt against all discipline, against all restrictions established for the fulfillment of a higher order of life.

§. 21. The Two Poles of World Order: The Fear of God and Full Humanity

The fear of God and full humanity are the twin poles of the ethical world order. The fear of God puts the seal of elevation on the individual man and the public condition. This elevation consists in being fully subsumed in the will of God and therefore in the unconditional fulfillment of higher commands without regard either for one's own life and well-being or the life and well-being of others. It elevates man above himself and all the powers and frailties of the earthly world. A picture of such elevation and unconditional devotion to God and, at least in accordance with our knowledge and our standard, virtually without humanity-inspired motivation, is found in the colossal appearance of Samuel in the Old Testament. Similar character, perhaps tempered by the spirit of the New Covenant, runs through the great men of <40> the Puritan church.[21] Humanity however is what provides the stamp of beauty, love, and kindness, the final consummation. The fear of God everywhere in dignity is the highest, in time the first. It begets humanity from itself. This is the eternal law, the course of history. Upon reaching maturity, however, it dare not close itself off, for in that case it becomes rotten and kills, it becomes Pharisaism in its manner of thinking, in institutions becomes a despotic and grotesque oppression. On the other hand, humanity dare not free itself from this, its true root. Otherwise it softens into the weakness of live and let live, into mutual interests merely regarding corporeal, earthly existence, the short-term indulgence of others to their long-term damage, as well as to that of the whole. Thus, love becomes the practice of worldly well-being, freedom the acclaim of arbitrariness. Following Kant, it is false humanity to make the man of appearance (homo phenomenon) the linchpin rather than man as he truly is (homo noumenon). For the public order, however, humanity freed from the fear of God leads on the one hand to fanaticism, as in the Revolution when the rights of man were imposed through the guillotine, and on the other hand, because human society can only be held together through God's ordinances, first to the slackening and then the dissolution of society.

---

[21] A similar elevation shows itself in the engrossment of men in higher ideas apart from a final relation to God, e.g., Roman civic virtue which did not even spare its own sons. But this virtue does not, as does Christian fear of God, give birth to humanity from itself as its other principle.

This is therefore the shadowy side of recent times along with its higher worth: that it only seeks man while being detached from what stands above man. Of the two parts through which the law is fulfilled – you shall love the Lord your God above all things, and your neighbor as yourself – it has arbi- <41> trarily picked out the second while ignoring the first, it has demolished the first of the two tables of the law while proposing to establish only the second. This is however contrary to the eternal ordinance. No building can stand when one removes the foundation, no tree can live when one lays the ax to the roots. The task of the times is therefore not the ongoing one-sided advance of humanity and the rights of man, but the restoration of the fear of God as the energetic principle in both hearts and public institutions, while in it and through it preserving humanity and the rights of man. This is the union of the truth of former times with contemporary times. It gives the testimonies of the one and the other principle their pure shape and their complete meaning and worth.

PART TWO: PROPERTY IN THE BROAD SENSE[22]

Chapter 1: Concerning Property* (Property in the Broad Sense) in General

§. 22. Property* as the Manifestation of Individuality

<43>Man is lifted out of the material base of his existence into the essence of the spirit. He is made from dust, but a divine breath has been breathed into him. For this reason he is on the one hand dependent on the material world outside of him, needing it for his maintenance and gratification; on the other hand he is elevated above it: it is for him a serviceable medium and material. In this manner, man is set in the creation as *lord*. The objects of the external world are allotted to him for the *satisfaction of his needs*, initially corporeal, and through them spiritual ones as well. However, in the *manner* of achieving satisfaction, that is, in the *arrangement of lifestyle and conduct*, the *personality* of man is to *actively involve itself*. For this reason man has, <44> from nature, power over things; for this reason in human common life there must also be *freedom* for each vis-à-vis everyone else *to do as one likes with those things;* things must be *enduringly and securely* subjected to one's will.

This is the basis for *property** in the broadest sense. Property is the material for the *manifestation of the individuality* of man. His innermost being reveals itself in the manner and measure in which he acquires and uses property. The manner of gaining a living, clothing, habitation, use for sensual enjoyment, for taste, art and science, for hospitality, liberality, goals of common utility,

---

[22] [This is Stahl's own definition of *Vermögen*, an umbrella term covering both property and contract. In the Roman legal tradition, property and contract together form the "law of things." In the German legal tradition, this concept of thing was developed into the concept of *Vermögen*, which roughly corresponds to "assets." Therefore, in the German tradition both property and contract are forms of assets. The implications of this understanding cannot be further explored here. In this translation the word *Vermögen* is translated as **property***, in order to distinguish it from property in the strict sense, which in German is *Eigentum*].

employment for acquisition and profit, for spiritual activity, for the contemplative life – this total way of life, resting on the foundation of property, is the image of man.

Property is however especially and primarily the material for the fulfillment of man's *ethical duties*. A man has particular *duties* that are *his alone*, which are not at the same time of others or of the community, duties stemming from his individual vocation and course of life, chiefly duties to his family. For this reason he must also have means which are *his alone*, in order that through their acquisition and use those duties can be fulfilled. In the manifestation of individuality and the fulfillment of special duties, for which property thus provides the necessary foundation, consists the activity of the personality of man.

Therefore property is not simply the satisfaction of human self-interest or the necessary means of maintenance, nor is it merely the purposeless rule over things; it is the material and means for a vocation, and therefore is itself a vocation.[23] Herein lies the ethical consecration of human relations to the goods **<45>**of the earth, that in their use the innermost character of men be made manifest, and that these goods be the means for them to uphold the family bond and family life. They are this however only by means of property.

§. 23. The Community of Goods

The community of goods, often contrasted with property as a higher, more ethical institution, does not answer to the purpose of property*. It does not even satisfy material needs, or if it does it does so insufficiently, and certainly not in a fair manner, because it neglects the incentive of production of goods, and values the lazy as highly as the productive. Above all, it eliminates the activity of personality, which is what truly consecrates property. With the distribution of goods by the community, the entire arrangement of life, it being built on goods, is likewise distributed by the community, and equally to each and every one. The human spirit hereby loses a portion of the material upon which it imprints its unique stamp, like taking from the artist the material he uses to express his thoughts. No less does it deny the fulfillment of ethical obligations to one's own.

---

[23] The expression lately arisen, that property is an *office* [Amt], is inappropriate. For office merely describes an activity for the entirety, for the public, while with the institution the first thing and basis is one's own satisfaction, by which free disposition is predominant; here the concept of office has no place.

Society, immediately or mediately, then provides for one's wife and children, comes to the aid of one's parents and relations. This in large part eliminates the ethical claims and activities of love from the holiest of bonds, and conversely eliminates ethical motivation from the relationship to goods. These goods then sink to the level of bare means for sensual maintenance and enjoyment.[24]

<46>The derivation of the community of goods from "Everything is common to those who love each other," as with Plato, rests on a misunderstanding. This is because the community of goods, being an expression of love, has to be a work of action (and thus of sharing), not a given condition. If the human will were immutable, which it should have been in accordance with its divinely created nature, then of course immutable love would have fomented the community of goods, albeit as a *perpetual act* (uninterrupted sharing). But because the human will is mutable, the community, that is the sharing of goods, can only be fleeting[25] and a community of goods as an institution, existing of itself apart from any action, would not make the human condition a whit more ethical.

The teaching of Christianity is based on this community by sharing, though by no means in opposition to the institution of property, and the first Christians did not at all live in a community of goods. "No one said of his own goods that they were his, but that they were everyone's in common" (Acts 4:32) refers to use, not to right. In order for Barnabas to lay the proceeds from his land at the Apostles' feet (Acts 4:37), he first had to own land and realize proceeds. Furthermore, such an act is praised as an exceptional example of love and not viewed as a Christian *duty*, as Peter expresses in his speech to Ananias (Acts 5:4): "you could have retained it (the land) in your possession, and when it was sold, it remained in your power." To the degree however that a propensity for community of goods is found in the early church, it differed fundamentally from the later political sects, namely the Communists. In the former case, the propensity was for those who <47> own goods to give; in the latter case there is the desire and the claim of the have-nots to take.

---

[24]Thus Aristotle (*Politics*, Book II, Ch. 3) rightly offers Plato the objection that he, in that he denies his "Guardians" separate property, also cuts them off from the virtue of generosity, communication to friends.

[25]In this sense the older writers are justified in viewing property as a consequence of the Fall.

A true community of goods is seen partially in the ancient world, and generally at the time of the initial development of peoples: for example, Oriental priests' landed property was considered common, and in Greek states a portion of the land often was allocated to all jointly. This community, which furthermore usually was restricted to certain objects, had, just as in the beginning, the lack of development of human individuality as its precondition – such a priest and even such a Greek citizen usually had their day-to-day activity in common with each other as well – and was based on the notion of common devotion to a higher calling (priestcraft, the state) in which the collective still formed an undivided unity – not on a bare equal claim to satisfaction on the part of separate individuals; and finally, its purpose was only bare maintenance, maintaining life in the highest degree of moderation, even to the point of an asceticism-oriented life, not to extend the luxurious pleasures of an overly cultured time to the poorer classes as well. This therefore can only be the calling of exceptional times and exceptional groups. Its significance is clearest in the monasteries. This same significance is also seen in the community of goods of the Pilgrim Fathers in New England. Earthly goods were far less important to them than the zeal to establish the kingdom of Christ. On the other hand, the movements for a community of goods in Europe after the Reformation – Thomas Munzer, the peasants' rebellion, the Levelers – were precursors of contemporary Communism, just as the political movements accompanying them were precursors of the Revolution. Then, it was the breaking of God's ordinances out of religious fanaticism; now, out of the lack of religion. **<48>**

§. 24. Inequality of Property*

The *inequality of property** is a necessary consequence of property. Whether it originally arose through occupation or distribution, equally or unequally, property must straightaway, in consequence of independence and thus independent destiny, lead to *inequality*. This is because property includes among its factors not simply nature and its available objects, which man to a certain degree can maintain in equal distribution; two other factors come into play, the *action and labor of man* and the *blessing of God*. These are however always and everywhere different. The one is industrious, the other is indolent, the one gathers, the other uses up. The one is a disciplined hunter, fisherman, shepherd, farmer, craftsman, the other performs these functions without talent. God also distributes his blessing differently. He determines that the one is born earlier than the other. He allows the one to succeed and the other to fail, He leads the one to the game and to the fish and not the other, He preserves for the one his fields and makes his herds fruitful while dispensing to the other hail and epidemics. Certainly such inequality of property*, which is to be attributed to the particular relations and gifts of each individual and the special leading of God, appertains to God's world order on earth and to the full development of the personality of men, similar to the way special gifts develop, and in like manner as all special destinies. In general therefore the legal basis of property as an institution is based in the vocation of men to actuate their personality; hence, presupposing this, the legal basis for specific property (of every person) lies in these three: the original inheritance through all generations reaching back to the initial distribution; the particular act of men (labor, saving or the lack thereof); and the dispensation of God. None of these three aspects should be **<49>** denied recognition and legal consequence.

In accordance with this, the *equality of goods* – while allowing separate property – is no command or goal of the legal order, as little as is the community of goods. It is contrary to justice that the industrious and the lounger, the thrifty and the profligate be put on the same line, and it is contrary to justice that the special gift of acquiring property* extended by God to a person and the special blessing extended by God to a person should bear no fruit to him. And in terms of outcome, it does not constitute a higher level of earthly condition that one person has just as much as another; but that, in the form and measure of property* there exist diversity and mutual supplementation as members of society.

The maintenance of the poor is by all means a command for the legal order as well (poor relief institutions, arrangement of contributions for the poor). The human community must in the extreme case provide for the life and existence of each and every individual. However, it does not do this by virtue of material solidarity in the goods of the earth, meaning that as soon as one has them in possession one must for that reason provide for another; but by virtue of the personal solidarity of the human race, in accordance with which, regardless of who possesses what, the race maintains its existence by personal performance and service. For this reason what is involved here is, firstly, not equality but only extreme need, and, secondly, even here not as property but as support, alms. This is not based on any entitlement on the part of the poor but on the ethical-legal duty of the community[26]; and he <50> who is unable to provide for oneself, be it his own fault or the special dispensation of God, is not owed full entitlement and full honor in the community.

§. 25. Equality of Distribution of Land

Somewhat different from the community or equality of goods is the concern to maintain each family in its landed property, and in the case of solely agrarian peoples, for each family to have landed property distributed to it. Although not a command, because of the impossibility of its unconditional implementation, it should nevertheless be a goal of the legal order. Here above all belongs the *Mosaic year of Jubilee*, the consequence of the idea that divine love extends to each family its own property, which human freedom cannot change without limit and contrary to this goal. Here belong the Germanic stipulations of inalienability, or difficulty of alienation, of landed property in the family. This is not in the least contrary to community or equality. Even with the institution of the Jubilee year, inequality remains in accordance with the increase of the family and the utilization of the land. These institutions are not an elimination but much rather the implementation of the idea of property, because they have in prospect nothing else than that property exist not merely in general (**in abstracto**) but with specific persons (**in concreto**).

Nor is the concern to combat excess inequality to be rejected. For example, Plato in his book *The Laws* and other writers listed by Aristotle taught that through the establishment of a maximum, or by some other means, a greater equality of property* should be promoted, and Greek institutions, especially in the Dorian states, were based on the same intention. Nevertheless, the goal here is more of a negative, compromising sort, that the one not receive too much at the start, rather <51> than being of a pure, exemplary character as with that other case, which is of an affirmative, independent provision, providing that each family for its own sake, apart from any comparison to others, have property to maintain or distribute.

Nowadays one unjustifiably seeks to abolish all institutions of this sort as being contrary to free private disposition. Although property itself is by nature a thing of free private disposition, the purpose for men to have property is still

[26]With regard to there being original legal duties and necessities which are not the consequence of the entitlement of another, see Book II [*Principles of Law*], §. 34.

a public one. Therefore, although no positive guidance of private disposition is admissible, the restriction of free private disposition, to wit, alienation, is so. None of these institutions are, like community of goods or equality of goods, contrary to the institution of property, but only modalities of the acquisition of and trade in property. Their further evaluation therefore forms part of the doctrine of national wealth (see Book IV).

§. 26. The Origin of Property

The vocation of man regarding property requires an initial distribution of the goods of the earth that are open to all. This was everywhere to take place in an orderly fashion. Thus, in the first human society this was to take place through allocation by forebears or through taking possession by reciprocal consent, as Abraham said to Lot: "if you decide to go to the left, I will go to the right; or if you decide to go to the right, I will go to the left." In this manner, the peoples were to divide the possession of the earth among themselves. However, in accordance with the character of the human race, from the beginning violence and struggle came in the place of amicable settlement.

The beginning of property among the peoples is therefore occupation of the land. This is based in the vocation of **<52>** peoples, which is to carry on an ordered ethical existence, the necessary condition of which is the exclusive possession of a certain land. The right of the people to its land is therefore based not on the mere act of taking possession, which is much rather only a precondition, but on the ordered ethical existence that it in fact establishes on that land, and on its power to maintain that existence. Therefore, the lack of an owner in the initial occupation is by no means the decisive factor.

The beginning of property among a people already in possession of its own order is not occupation through individuals but distribution through the ruling authority. For all property in the final analysis is derived from landed property. The material of enjoyment and labor are the product of the ground, and the pasturing of livestock and the hunting of game presupposes property in land. Among nearly all peoples landed property is originally divided out rather than left to arbitrary occupation. The Promised Land was conferred to the Jews by tribes and families, in Greek states the citizens kept the landless out of the state, and in Rome private ownership of land took place through assignation; the kings and princes of the Germanic peoples distributed conquered land as fiefs among their followers. This is in accordance with the essence of property. In its initial origin, it is not grounded in one's own power but on authority, it is not something attained but something received. On the other hand, its independence begins immediately; the initial distribution is irrevocable, and upon this basis property is further acquired through the particular act and destiny of each individual. <53>

§. 27. The Ultimate Justification of Property

The law-idea of property is as original as that of contract or the state itself; for this reason, the validity of property by no means presupposes either a contract to that effect or the state. Something different than contract or the state is however a *community of legal consciousness and observance.* This is by all means a precondition for the realization of property, because without it the law-idea of property would lack the specificity necessary to its realization, e.g., how is property acquired, through occupation or only first through usucapion? And how is it lost? etc. This is however no less true for every other legal institution, especially contract and the state itself. The controversy concerning whether property is binding in itself or only in consequence of agreement is hereby settled by reference to the fact that no law-idea (rational law) is in force in itself but must first be positivized (Book II, ch. 2).

§. 28. Property* Extends to Acts

The object of property* is first of all *material things* [Sachen], the right to which is *property* in the strict or technical sense. However, the acts and performances [Leistungen] of other persons are also the object of property* because they generate effects in the material world, and therefore – be it through the bestowal of things, be it even direct – they serve to provide satisfaction no less than do material things. In accordance with the general significance of property* – in which personality freely manifests itself in the manner of satisfaction, in the shape given to lifestyle – control and the power of disposition are required with regard to these performances as well, in like manner to material things; here in particular, this is the security by which they can be counted on, so as to be able to appoint <54> one's life. This guaranteed power of disposition over another's actions is the concept of *obligation* (**obligatio**) and is the other part of property* besides property, to be distinguished from bare factual performance (**datio**). In this manner, one person serves the other as material, as a thing, but only for individual outward actions. The person himself and the inner personal bonds or outward expressions of the same cannot be the object of property. The object of obligation is therefore neither the person of another nor the performance directly, considering that there can be no immediate disposal, even factually, over performance; rather, the object is the performance of another through the *instrumentality of his will*, thus this will itself as bound, in order by means thereof to be able to bring about performance according to place and time; this is the *legal bond* (**vinculum juris**). Therefore, the obligation always firstly has a *future* object in mind, and when this moves into the present, in fulfillment, it also spells the obligation's termination (**solutio**). In accordance with the solidarity of men, there exists (**potentia**) a general mutual capacity for performance and therefore also of obligation. On the other hand, in line with their freedom, in order for obligation to make a real appearance (**actu**) there must be a special occurrence (**causa**), as a rule voluntary acceptance; accordingly, the obligation is always a bond between specific persons (creditor and debtor).

As a result, the total idea of property* is this: the earth with its goods (including human performances) is the substrate of human satisfaction, realized however by means of guaranteed special entitlement of individuals, the goal being the free shaping of individual life. In this manner there arise just as many centers of property* spheres as there are people, the material of which is partly things, partly legal obligations to perform on the part of other men.

<55> Property* is however typified by property because material things are the sole indispensable and the most significant means of satisfaction, while obligations are dissolved in the bestowal of things or, in more developed social conditions, virtually always find a complete equivalent in things. Property is therefore the central point to which all other property* rights relate. All property* however has to do with goods of general and exchangeable value. This lies in the nature of the matter, it being corporeal means. The representative of general and exchangeable value is *money*. Only that which has money value can be an object of property.

§. 29. The Twofold Purpose of Property: Satisfaction and Control

The purpose (τέλος) of property* is dual: *satisfaction* through external objects and *control* over them in order *freely to give shape to one's way of life;* however, the two are inseparable and stand only in relation to the other.

Satisfaction of needs is the constructive impulse of the law of property*; through it the various institutions comprising that law take shape, e.g. that there be property, servitudes, lien, purchase, exchange, hire, etc. However, the general character displayed by all its institutions is *control*, the free, secure disposal by the individual, unconditional subjective entitlement. The former determines the shape of the institution, the latter the role of the person in it. Therefore *rights* are the *only* content of the law of property*, duties only as the consequence of those rights; external matter is merely passive, it imposes no commitment, and the rights here concerned are freely disposable. This is its peculiar character, which is found in no sphere of law outside it.

<56> The character of control in property* rights is the general requirement that cannot be lacking in a legal system; but the excellence of a legal system consists in satisfaction being made possible in the most various and complete manner, while leaving this character inviolate. The older legal structures were mainly determined by the consideration of satisfaction as the first and natural goal of property. The idea of free unconditional secure control first makes its decisive appearance in the Roman law, but in such a one-sided and rigid manner that the initial goal of satisfaction or utility (**utilitas**) often led, for example, to legal transactions being seen merely in terms of the bare will and its justification, not according to their inner purpose of gratification; for this reason, for example, no exception of deception or repayment could stand against a stipulation. This was offset in later development (**praetor, Caesar**). In German law, both principles permeate each other. Thus, in contrast to the former, property* in its full organic correlation is viewed as an institution [Anstalt] of human common satisfaction, and therefore the law of property* is not conceived apart from the relation to the creation of property*. While the Roman law conceived the world of goods simply as pre-existing, the objects of which are appropriated and mutually distributed by individuals through their will, Germanic law views goods likewise as being produced continually anew by the human community, according to which the consideration of this production and its stimulation has to be a decisive aspect likewise for the manner of appropriation and distribution. As a result, the vocation of estates, in accordance with their manner of earning a living and the political position based on this (the landowner in general and the nobility in particular, followed by the industrial and commercial classes, etc.), has its influence on the law of property*. This is an advantage of Germanic law over Roman law. The Romans brought the law of **<57>** property to fulfillment simply with reference to itself; but the relation of the law of property to the economy and to political conditions must be granted essential influence, in the spirit of Germanic law, although in terms of its content this naturally must change with changes in the economy and political conditions themselves, and with the changed position of classes.

§. 30. False Justifications of Property: Kant, Hegel, Locke

The older school of natural law taught an original community of goods (**communio primaeva**); in this concept it usually confounded the legal establishment of common usage and the factual condition of general arbitrary seizure. Property however it conceived as the consequence of a mutual contractual establishment.[27] This continued up until Kant, who by contrast deduced property as an original right of the person, actually simply from the idea of freedom and the will, and thus also with the meaning of a *purposeless power* over the thing. The acquisition of property according to Kant is therefore the act by which a person subjects the thing to his will – *seizure*. Hegel follows him in this.[28] Both men merely consider the power of people over the thing, not their dependence on the thing. Not only is the first aspect of property, the satisfaction of needs, hereby nullified or contrary to nature made into something secondary, but even the other aspect, free disposal and control, is not conceived in its true signifi-
<58> cance. The meaning of property does not lie in its being an expression of human freedom, that man has a passive object at his command and in so doing celebrates his triumph as a person (this is much more merely the factual power of mankind over nature, not the legal power of a person over against another) – but that by means of this command he freely gives shape to his way of life and in this way manifests his individuality.

Besides this theory of Kant's and Hegel's, there is the fundamentally divergent one of Locke's. Locke deduces property from *need and utility*, because man, as experience teaches, cannot exist without property, and the acquisition of property is therefore to him the act by which a person produces a thing useful

[27]For more on this see Vol. I, p. 145 [*The Rise and Fall of Natural Law*, pp. 126ff.].

[28]"The rational in property does *not* lie in *satisfaction of needs*, but in this, that the bare subjectivity of personality is subsumed" (*Natural Law* [Naturrecht – a.k.a. *Philosophy of Law*], §. 41). This selfsame property is further described as "the reality of my freedom in an external thing," which just for that reason "is a poor reality" [eine "schlechte Realität sey"]; see §. 39 as well.

to human need – *labor*. Here we have the reverse conception: the higher meaning of property, the activity of personality, is completely disregarded. The former theory of property is the consequence of the rationalistic viewpoint, the latter the empirical viewpoint.[29] Neither deduction provides an answer to the question as to what it is that gives a person the right over against others to take possession of a thing for himself or to process a thing for himself.

[29]See Vol. I, p. 317 [*The Rise and Fall of Natural Law*, pp. 259ff.].

Chapter 2: The Communist-Socialist Repudiation of Property

§. 31. The Rationale Behind the Repudiation of Property

<59> During the entire development of legal philosophy, agreement reigned concerning the necessity and justice of property, with opinions differing only about the manner of its foundation. In our day a doctrine has arisen and achieved power in the world putting this necessity and justice itself in question – *Communism* and *Socialism.*

In terms of their goals, Communism and Socialism indeed are a system of economics and not law, but nevertheless they are based on a certain overarching foundational principle of law, the *repudiation of property*. Apart from this it must a priori appear inadmissible to set the social condition on a foundation opposed to property.

Within this new doctrine, there exists, apart from the many subordinate deviations, a foundational difference in terms of economic viewpoint, finding expression in the dual appellation; namely, that Communism is a community of goods while Socialism is only a community of economic activity (as further explained in Book IV of this volume [*The Doctrine of State and the Principles of State Law,* §. 22]). Just so, there exists a fundamental divergence in legal perspective. To wit, the one denies property in the objects given by nature, the other by contrast denies all property plain and simple, thus also in those objects which one's own labor or special competence and ability in labor provides him; one may have a particular <60> right in virtually nothing. So Fourier aims for a distribution of the yield attained by society according to the standard of labor and talents which each has contributed in society, and therefore allows labor and talent and that which they effectuate as property for each individual, for the sake of which they have a claim to a higher share of consumption. By contrast, Proudhon rejects any preference for talents and quality of labor, determining the value of objects merely in terms of the *time* of labor; accordingly, men have no more property in their own abilities and skills, these are common property, only the time applied to labor is one's own. Finally, Louis Blanc goes beyond that, establishing that the yield of social labor be distributed merely in accordance with *need*, so that the laborer who is also the most gifted, competent, and assiduous, nevertheless receives the least if he needs the least, e.g., if he has no children, and vice versa. This is the culmination. According to this, one simply has *nothing left* which is his own.

Indeed, both of these divergent legal viewpoints correspond to both divergent economic viewpoints, albeit not in complete correspondence. Babeuf and the committed Communists, although they do not state the question clearly, in essence nevertheless go as far as the complete denial of property, in that they do not even allow for the development of special talent, while conversely the entire national-economic school called into being by Fourier goes only as far as mere partial repudiation of property.[30] The entire Communist-Socialist school then is united in this, that there can be no property in **<61>** things in the true sense, in objects which are the mere gifts and products of nature; the only difference in viewpoint consists in whether property can exist in the products of one's own labor, in the values created by man himself.

§. 32. Proudhon

The total repudiation of property is stated by Proudhon in his celebrated book: "What Is Property?" (qu'est ce que la proprieté?). The answer he gives is: property is theft (la proprieté c'est le vol). This rendition is however likewise the only attempt at all at a scientific justification of the unlawfulness of property, which is presupposed by the entire Socialist-Communist orientation.

Proudhon's method of proof is to demonstrate the unlawfulness of all titles of property:

One cannot derive property from *occupation,* for the arbitrariness of the seizure could not justify any right, and the possession itself could at most command respect only as long as the possessor is on it, and only as far as he exercises it personally and directly, just in the theater nobody can occupy more places than he occupies with his body; one cannot derive property from *labor,* because the authorization to labor already presupposes ownership of the thing, and the

[30] In the distribution of the social product Fourier does take into account capital brought in, but with regard to the future such is only to be the product of prior labor; for the initial beginning, Fourier only allows it by connivance, because to be consistent Fourier cannot recognize property as such, it deriving from the current unlawful condition of civilization. Nor does Fourier at any time allow for property as a separate object of labor.

labor only creates a higher value of the thing, not the thing itself; one cannot derive property from *positive law* (i.e., as the elders taught, from a contractual stipulation at the founding of the state society), for positive law may not order anything that is not justified in itself, i.e. contrary to reason and justice. Since property can in no way be justified according to this, it is illegal, and for this very reason it is a withholding of the equal share that belongs to the rest, i.e., theft.

His entire method of proof rests however on a flawed line of reasoning. He demonstrates the injustice of property by arguing that no title of acquiring property (occupation, labor, contractual establishment) can justify that property. But the title of acquisition is not the basis of property; property is the basis of its title of acquisition. It certainly is foolish to say that while men can take possession of things, can cultivate them, for this reason there must be property; this is what Proudhon refutes, and he doesn't have much trouble doing so. On the contrary: occupation, cultivation, prescription and the like, all are titles of acquisition under the presupposition and on the grounds that, apart from them, the necessity and justice of property is established in and of itself. If property in land, in game etc. does not exist on other grounds, occupation of the same does as little to ground property as does the occupation of a spot in the theater or on the lake shore. However, when property in land etc. is necessary and justified in itself in accordance with nature and the vocation of man, **<62>** there must then be actions to acquire it, from which follows acquisition through occupation, cultivation and the like, from the lawfulness of property and not the reverse. The final and decisive question is therefore whether property in itself is a postulate of human nature, the ethical condition of the human race, and this question, upon which everything else turns, is left untouched by Proudhon. Therefore, while he is able to refute the usual method of justifying property (from the will and the act of volition of man) – something which had already been done before him, in this book – he did not refute property itself, and in fact did not even bring up the question of property.

§. 33. Considerant

The straightforward denial of property in the objects of nature is expounded with the most awareness by Considerant,[31] roughly in the following manner:

Everything that nature grants is a common good, belongs to all people undividedly (**pro indiviso**), and no single person can have separate property in it in preference to another. Nor can one generation in preference to another. On the other hand, what man produces through his labor is his creation, is not granted as such by nature, and is therefore his *own* for himself and for his heirs. Those currently possessionless[32] can therefore claim the soil of the earth, the landed property, from the possessors, for they have the same right to it. But this only pertains to the soil itself, thus as it was originally by nature, not what the present owners or their ancestors have made of the soil through their labor, its improvement, thus not the soil in its present increased value. This is where the difficulty arises: if the present landholders maintain their exclusive possession, it is an injustice to the possessionless, because the latter are deprived of a gift of nature; on the other hand, if they have to share their landholding with the latter, it is an injustice to the possessors because it means that their labor and that of their ancestors, i.e., their actual property, is taken away from them. The rectification is then the *guarantee of labor*. Because the soil can no longer be kept separate from the utilization of the soil, the possessors should keep the soil but guarantee the others an income in exchange for labor, i.e., employment and wages. This is compensation to them for their claim to the bounty of nature, the soil, the more so as the soil never nourishes without work, and, if it could be restored to its original condition and given to them according to their share, they would also have the labor of hunting, fishing, fruit gathering.

At first glance, this more moderate doctrine seems quite obvious, as if it hit the center of truth and strikes the right balance between the old social order and

---

[31] See the start of Stein's *Socialism and Communism*, p. 205. Considerant is entirely the pupil of Fourier; cf. his *Destinée Sociale*.

[32] ["Besitzlosen" – this word is commonly translated as "dispossessed", but the literal translation is possession (Besitz) + less (losen). "Dispossessed" implies previous possession that is subsequently removed, and thus introduces a value judgment that is not in the original, for "possessionless" makes no statement about previous possession.]

the new Communist system. But it, too, completely falls apart under closer examination.

According to its own principles, it cannot be carried out at all without admitting the bankruptcy of justice. For the just claim of the possessionless cannot be determined according to it: how much is the value of the original land, how much is its improvement through labor? How much do the current possessors have to give up for what they stole from the rest through consumption of common property (e.g., wood)? Conversely, how much is owed to the present possessionless, since they themselves or their ancestors may have had plenty and were spendthrift, through equality of consumption? And just compensation for the claim of the possessionless is likewise neither ascertainable nor grantable. The guarantee of labor, which only secures their meager subsistence, cannot be a substitute for withholding a share of the land, which would give them an object of labor and thus the possibility of acquiring similar independent property.

Furthermore, the doctrine is inconsistent. For if the gift of nature, namely the soil, is a common good, it was not for the present possessors and their ancestors to work it and appropriate the increase in value, as Proudhon rightly points out.

But all this impracticability and inconsistency is based on the fact that the basic idea itself – the separation of natural gifts and human labor – is untenable. These two factors of wealth are inextricably linked. All human labor has the gift of nature either as raw material or as reward. If it were so that the gifts of nature belong to man in common for all time, man's labor could find no raw material, for no one can work for his own appropriation from what is common, and it could find no reward, for what is common could be not provided as a reward to anyone who accepts and benefits from the labor. Conversely, if appropriation through human labor is to be permissible, then appropriation of the natural objects themselves must necessarily be permissible from the outset. And that the gifts of the earth, other than sun and air, require the mediation of human labor to serve for subsistence, is a proof that they are destined to be property.

Finally, from the outset it is an arbitrary prerequisite to declare ownership of the gifts of nature to be inadmissible. Considerant and those who stand by his standpoint have not even attempted to provide a proof for this; Proudhon alone attempted it, but failed to produce it.

§. 34. The True Rationale: Antipathy to God's Dispensation

The true motivation for the denial of property by Communism and Socialism, either in general or at least regarding the gifts of nature, does not lie in the weak reasoning of Proudhon and the like but goes much deeper, to a frame of mind, namely *antipathy to God's dispensation.* In fact man does not desire to receive anything from God's Providence and does not wish to recognize what one's neighbor receives through God's Providence. Nature appears to be a **<63>** storehouse of goods not from God as Lord distributing them but simply from men, with the one man being as much lord over them as the other, and with the totality of man, society, distributing them in terms of equality.

It is God who allots to each man his portion, his particular talent and his particular acquisition; upon this is based specific property for every person, as stated above (§. 24). If property is not based on this, only *arbitrariness* and *coincidence* remains: arbitrariness, that the one person takes possession and wishes to maintain it for himself, caprice, that the one person has the opportunity to take possession before the other. However, neither arbitrariness nor caprice can justify an advantage in the goods of the earth, to which in fact all men by nature must turn for their support. For this reason, when the Providence of God is not recognized as the legal ground of all property, the hunter or fisherman must surrender his prey: game and fish are by nature there for everyone; the rich harvest or the fruitful herd must be thrown in for the general use, and even the special gift by which the one has a sharper eye or a steadier hand extends him no right to them, because it is a means of supporting everyone. Communism therefore was justified in objecting against legal philosophy from Grotius up until Hegel, that property in the end is founded merely on the will of man, and it is justified over against current society because the latter, like Communism, is ready to free itself from God. But to be consistent the Providence of God must be resisted just as strongly with regard to peoples as to individual persons. If the proletariat in France were right to claim their original portion from the rich, so are the Laplanders justified in laying a claim against the French people, that they be pushed no further back into that unfruitful region while the French reside on the banks of the gleaming, flowing Loire, given that nature and the earth were given for all equally.

<64> As is the case with all efforts at all times to achieve a community of goods, the error of Communism therefore consists in general in the denial of the ethical meaning of property and the illusion regarding the ethical value of the community of goods, but in particular it consists – and this is its innermost distinguishing characteristic – in the non-recognition of the leading of God in the distribution of goods. This latter point is the godlessness of Communism and at the same time the way in which it violates law: because that which through God's leading becomes a man's, is his most holy right.

Chapter 3: Real Rights and Personal Rights

§. 35. The Twofold Rights of Property*

<65> With the character of property* as unconditional entitlement to an external object established, the law of property* divides itself into two classes of rights: *real rights* and *personal rights* [dingliche und persönliche Rechte].[33]

In accordance with that character, the real right [das Recht auf die Sache] must of necessity be prosecutable against anyone who withholds it from the possessor, whether honest or dishonest, whether obtained against consideration or not [lukrativen oder onerosen] – **actio in rem**; the personal right, on the other hand, is just as necessarily prosecutable, but against the specific person who is obligated – **actio in personam**. If performance is a pure act or payment, it is self-evident that no third party is obligated to it. But even where performance consists in providing or relinquishing specific things, it is not the thing directly but its provision that is the object of the right, and therefore it is not the possessor of the thing who can be held to it but only the one obligated to performance. This is the strict implementation of Roman law, which Kant [34] for that reason considers to be the only possible one philosophically. <66>

§. 36. Satisfaction as Principle of Property

The legal structure may however also proceed predominantly simply from the other principle of property*, satisfaction, and thus realize retributive justice or equity rather than protective justice. For the relation of a person to an object (material thing [Sache]) is not something unconditional and thus not a standard to weigh all further events and acts, but the reverse, the events are treated at every moment in and for themselves and only thereafter is the relation of the participants to the thing determined. It is not who has the right to the thing but who, under these conditions taken together, has merited the more preferential treatment which is what is decisive to such an approach. It views whether some-

---

[33] Here in the law of property*, in accordance with its particular nature (§. 29), is precisely the area within which the diversity of objects of entitlement is a chief determining principle for legal norms.

[34] *Doctrine of Law,* p. 103.

one truthfully or insincerely, fairly or unfairly, cautiously or less cautiously has acted in the event in question, whether one's condition was affected by the insincerity of another, for example whether the honest buyer or pledgee merits protection rather than the incautious owner, whether the one who orders merchandise at an earlier period is to be favored before the one who orders later but who is nevertheless put in possession by the seller without taking that obligation into account, and the like. The withholding of a thing is in this case an injustice not simply because it belongs to another; everything depends on the event as to how one came upon the thing in question, and only thereby is settled to whom it belongs; and vice versa, things owed to us by another may be claimed from a third party according to the event by which the latter came to acquire it. In this manner real rights are absorbed through events among third parties, and personal rights are prosecuted in the manner of real rights. In fact, if consistently implemented the distinction between real rights and personal rights entirely disappears, because the concept of an un- <67> conditional right to an object itself disappears; all is resolved into a continuous allocation of objects in accordance with passing events and acts.[35]

§. 37. Control as Principle of Property

This viewpoint – which we should like to call the pure *utility principle* – possessed a significant power in ancient legal systems prior to the Roman. Certainly it was nowhere exclusively implemented, the principle of secure control being

[35]In this fashion a legal system is conceivable in which the actual concept of property, the right to a material thing, is entirely lacking as a positive one [ein positiver] and is only indirectly protected through prohibitions of actions which in themselves are illegal, as for example one who secretly appropriates a material thing, one who illegally sells it, one who finds it and does not announce the fact, etc., would have to restore it to the one who until then had it. In this manner property is protected through mere claims [Forderungen]. An institution of this sort in our legal system is **possessio** [possession], and thus the fruitless attempt to allot a place for it in the classification of real and personal rights. The **bonae fidei possessio** is certainly a real right, but one which in its further development is subject to that viewpoint of events and thus relativity, as for example that the one who earlier received something from the same originator [Autor] has priority over the one currently possessing it, from which as well the reservation of the praetor to himself decide in the case of conflict.

too deeply grounded in the essence of the law of property*.[36] The Roman legal system, in accordance with its character of unconditional entitlement regarding an object, brought the distinc- <68> tion between real and personal rights to clear consciousness and fixed implementation; it makes up the face as it were of the Roman law of property*. It alone guarantees the security of rights which we have characterized as the ethical idea of property*. Furthermore, it alone can be harmoniously carried out, while the contrary way, because of the vagueness of its principles, always leads to conflicts both between various claims independent of each other and various equally relevant considerations. The Roman law also has institutions based in part on the former point of view, but, at least in its original shape, it had in certain degree separated them from the legal system proper, based on magistrates' protection, for instance the **actio publiciana** and in a certain sense as well the **possessio** as a protection in things relatively dependent on personal events, and vice versa the **actio ad exhibendum, quod metus causa, Pauliana** as the prosecution of claims to obligation against third-party, usually underhand, possessors of the thing in question.

Germanic law, although equally based on secure entitlement, nevertheless did not implement this distinction to this level of consistency. The Germanistic concept of "Gewehre" often has the character of *relativity*. Regarding movables, my priority ahead of the third-party possessor depends on the manner in which I lost possession of the thing, whether against my will or in accordance thereof, in which case my incautious confidence comes at my own expense; regarding immovables it depends on whether I myself am still in possession, whether I have been so for a year and a day, whether my opponent or his testator was present at the time of the transfer to me, whether he was absent or present during the established time period when I acquired the preference, or, as the case may

[36]So for example according to the lawbook of the Manu, the sale or donation not made by the true owner is not valid as sale or donation (§. 299, in Hüttner, p. 279), although under conditions the one demanding reinstatement [der Vindikant] must reimburse half the selling price (cf. Schönemann, p. 490), when not the thing itself. However, according to Attic law (Heffter), the mortgagee has priority over the true owner and the honest possessor retains the thing when its originator [Autor] pleads for him against the owner. In this manner, that viewpoint obviously emerges here. Even the form of contested inheritance [Diadikasie] for such cases is an outgrowth of it.

be, whom did the same liege lord first enfeoff. Even if these determinations are connected with procedural arrangements [prozessualischen Einrichtungen], this **<69>** nevertheless at the least demonstrates a lack of the concept of absolute entitlement. For this reason, even now in the wake of the reception of the Roman law individual modifications and exceptions have been made in the fixed foundation of the Roman distinction between real and personal rights, which are appropriate in this detail and restriction, although in general and as a principle of the entire legal system – which is what the judge must implement absent exceptional determinations – the Roman unconditionality of entitlement deserves the preference.[37]

[37]For example "Hand muss Hand wahren" [only the direct acquirer of property might be held responsible]; determinations regarding public auctions; determination that the first buyer has priority over the second, to whom it was conveyed, when the latter knew of the initial purchase; purchase does not nullify tenancy, apart from judicial sale; the owner, when he demands the surrender of his property [wenn er vindicirt], must reimburse the purchase price or the amount of debt to the buyer or the pawnbroker; and the like. Such determinations, which are found in German local laws and municipal statutes, and in particular in our Prussian civil code, are as *separate determinations* more or less appropriate. Should one however desire to treat the here underlying notions as the *principle of legislation*, which with new legislative regulations and judicial decisions determines new cases, it would in the end threaten the security of property. In this sense, for example, the determinations of the Prussian civil code already in the case of unclear clauses are often expanded there, such that even the *statutory* lien of the landlord extends also to such introduced properties which are the property not of the tenant but of a third party.

§. 38. The Unity of Real and Personal Rights

Real rights and personal rights nevertheless also have a *deeper unity*. This is founded on the one hand on the general purpose of property*, satisfaction, which is the purpose of both, hence noncompliance on the part of the defendant in itself could not lead to a verdict of compensation, it first re- <70> quired special "Sponsionen," and vice versa, only the person of the debtor was liable for personal obligations, not his goods. The law of pledge, however, the most decisive manifestation of the transition between personal and real rights, was lacking to the Romans, who first learned of the true law of pledge (**hypotheca**) from the Greeks; the **pignus** of the older law had the effect of pledge only de facto, the **fiducia** only indirectly. In the later development of the Roman law and even more decisively in Germanic law, unity came to the fore. The latter in particular contains legal relations in accordance with which a real right, i.e., a property* claim attached to a thing, is exercised and completed in personal performance, and just for this reason, on the other hand, a real right is inseparably joined to the duty of personal performance – *services in kind* [Reallasten].[38]

---

[38]The payable performance is thus a personal claim; it does not pass to the successor as past due, but it can be made into a real claim through entry of title in the real estate register [Ingrossation]. To subsume the relation under a Roman type of action [Klagegattung], as for instance under the **actiones in rem scriptae**, as has been attempted, is therefore impossible. That rights of this character for the most part have sprung from public law is not relevant here; after all, they have acquired a property*-legal character.

Chapter 4: The Law of Material Things [Sachenrecht]

§. 39. Property in Things: Full and Partial

<71> The character of property* as free control and disposal requires a legal institution by which the person has *total power* over a thing. Fragmentation allowing the one to do this, the other to do that with the same thing, does not answer to it; rather, the thing must serve one person fully and completely as the object of his will, so that he freely disposes over it. This total power [Gesammtbefugniß] is *property.*

The purpose of property* further requires that every satisfaction be vouchsafed, even such legal institutions in which particular powers are detached from the total power of property and transferred to someone other than the owner, equally as an immediate and unconditional right to the thing, as a real right, especially the following:

1. The value of a piece of land often depends on certain provisions [Gewährungen] on the part of neighboring property [Nachbargutes] (forbearances or allowances for undertakings), and therefore in order to secure or increase this value, place must be made for the right to this undertaking in terms of the law of material things – *easements* or *praedial servitudes.*

2. Familial succession or the wish of the testator requires that the use of a thing or property be maintained for someone <72> (for example the widow) for that person's lifetime without the thing or the property being removed from the actual heir forever; for this reason the use of all or certain usages must be made available without being able to create the right of disposal in the manner of real rights – *usufruct* or *personal servitudes.* This is the motive upon which the institution of personal servitudes is based, which once formed are also extended entirely naturally through a contractual arrangement either for a shorter period or for life.[39]

---

[39]Real and personal servitudes have no inner affinity. Their summation under the single concept of servitudes in Roman law is based on pure historical grounds, that originally they were the only **jura in re** known to the civil law. What is common between them,

3. The security of the creditor and therefore also the credit of the borrower requires that the former in future must be able to count on the satisfaction through things that at present belong to the debtor – for this reason the right of possible alienation of a thing in order to cover a debt must be able to be arranged in terms of real rights – *lien* [Pfandrecht], etc. In accordance with the above, however, these rights are not independent, so that the object lies in the middle, between the one <73> with more and the one with less powers; they are restrictions, burdens on property – *real rights in material things owned by another* [dingliche Rechte an fremder Sache].

Finally, the exceptional nature of landed property, the yield of which is based on a dual factor, land and labor, the former of which moreover in the Germanic legal system often is granted by a higher authority, a representative of public power, entails peculiar legal relations:

1. a distribution of rights to each in accordance with their various contributions, be it in the form of a real right to a thing owned by another, *perpetual lease* [Emphyteuse], be it as truly *shared property*, the latter however not as a direct fragmentation of property right but rather as an organic relation among the participants;

---

attachment to a certain subject, in the former case the plot of land, in the latter the person, from which follows the nontransferability of the same, is in itself already hardly significant given the essential dissimilarity between land and person, and has even fewer other juridical consequences. Outside of the maxims valid for all **jura in re aliena** (e.g., **in faciendo consist. nequit – res propria nemini servit.**) they have nothing in common. So for example the **civiliter uti**, the **causa continua** etc. of real servitudes do not apply to personal servitudes, nor do the bailment and encumbrance of personal servitudes apply to real servitudes; the manner of origin and production, the treatment of possession and prescription is entirely different for each according to the necessity of the matter. Usufruct has much more in common with emphyteusis than with the **jus viae**, **actus**, **ne luminibus**, etc. It is by no means any inner ground by which these heterogenous rights are grouped over against the other **jura in re** as a common concept.

2. rights to land and soil, realized in a tax [Abgabe] on the possessor – *services in kind*.[40]

§. 40. Components of Property Rights

Property therefore is the right (the legal authority) over a thing in *its totality*. It is however for this reason the *general* and *complete* right to the thing, that is, it contains every power not specially removed, while on the contrary restricted rights have no authority other than what is expressly provided; and presumption contends for the unrestricted character of property. Furthermore, it is the *original* and *independent* right to the thing, while <74> other real rights assume property and an owner which restrict them. Finally, it is an *exclusive* right to the thing, while many other real rights held by various entitled persons may exist in the same thing independently of each other, for example praedial servitudes.

The powers contained in property, in accordance with both motives of the law of property* (§. 29), are of a dual form: rights of use and of disposal. The former involves use and usufruct, the latter concerns changes in the thing, in its substance or in its legal relation. However, because satisfaction is the initial motive of property*, the right of disposal, as was rightly emphasized by Hegel, cannot exist when all use is removed from it (**nuda proprietatis**). In fact, use should only be removed in restricted degree, namely either in restricted extent (for example praedial servitudes) or restricted duration (for example personal servitudes).

§. 41. Forms of Joint Ownership

Both natural organic bonds between persons and those artificially formed for a purpose, even if it be for the purpose of property* itself (marriage, agnation, community, common family property [Ganerbschaft], joint stock corporation) also exercise, by means of their power over persons, a power over those persons' position with regard to the thing, and thereby effectuate a joint right held by these persons to the thing, in determinate shapes. This was properly appreciated by Germanic law, and from it stems a series of institutions of this character, for

[40] Thus the *real purpose* [reale Bestimmung] of property* is to vouchsafe every satisfaction, from which arises the system of real rights, not, as Hegel constructs it, the *logical categories* of general (value) and particular (determinate thing) and the like. The former is only the proper principle of its construction.

which the Germanists developed the concept of "*shared property*" [Gesammteigentums]. The innermost meaning of this concept is that it is owed to people, to individuals, not however in their isolation as in Roman property but in their **<75>** organic unity; this had as a consequence that both, the organic bond (the community) and the individual, are vested with rights. It is hereby opposed on the one hand to the Roman doctrine of the legal person, which entitles merely the whole (bond, unity), and on the other hand to the Roman doctrine of joint property which entitles merely the individual. In it, the right-bearers are entitled to the property only jointly, not separately, and thus are not entitled to a determinate proportion over which they have unrestricted disposal. This is even true of community of goods in marriage, which comes closest to Roman joint property. But the participants have a direct part as individuals in the right; the latter does not belong to a legal person constructed from the participants only to be entirely separated from them; and therefore they may, in accordance with their specific relation, have individual powers of property as a separate independent right, as for example the shareholder having the right to sell his shares. In what manner the right of the whole is related to the right of the individual depends on the specific nature of each of these organic bonds. It is everywhere a specific individual articulation of the institution. For this reason no practical consequences for individual institutions can be derived from the mere concept of shared property; the practical significance of the concept as a general one consists much more in the negative sense of exclusion of principles regarding Roman joint property and property of the legal person.

Even so, the German-legal concept of *divided property*, which is not to be derived from the mere relation to the object, is based rather in the higher organic relation of persons, whom the object can serve in that relation as well as it can in their isolation. The Romanizing dismantling of this concept into property with **jus in re aliena** – with actual ownership ascribed either to the over- or under- **<76>** proprietor – would destroy the unity and innermost principle of this legal institution, it being based in the legal relation between the persons, which often first determines the property relation. For example, fealty or subjection, be it only for own collection of levies, or dismissal [Privation] which nevertheless rules out the devolution of usufruct to the owner [Konsolidation], etc., cannot possibly be construed from a **dominium** with **jus in re**. Nor can **dominium directum** be conceived as a mere political overarching power, because its consequences are too significantly private-legal and pecuniary for that. The capacity of the law of property* to be determined by such higher personal bonds is generally an advantage of Germanic law. Whether precisely *these* personal bonds will continue to exist in the future is another question, the answer to which it is not here the place to give.

§. 42. The Acquisition of Property

The *acquisition* of property everywhere presupposes the will of the acquirer, the *property intent*, property* being an affair [Sache] of freedom. However, this will alone does not yet yield property; there must first be a *ground of acquisition*, that is the effectuation of a specific relation to the object, be it direct, be it indirect through other people, through which the preference is gained ahead of others with the same will. The various sorts of such grounds of acquisition are based on the notion that things [Sachen] have the purpose of serving the human race, that is the peoples, as a whole for their preservation and satisfaction, and yet have the purpose of entitling individuals to specific rights, precisely in accordance with their actions and destinies. In line with this, property is primevally derived partly from the community and partly from the deeds of acquisition of individ-
<77> uals; and from then on it is partly the circulation of that property, partly the acquisition of new property which perpetually takes place, with the former however only occurring through acts or legal relations of persons. From this is derived the following system of grounds of acquisition:

§. 43. Original Acquisition

Acquisition of property is of two main sorts: *original* and *derivative* acquisition, that is, independent founding of property merely through an act or procedure of the acquirer, and derivation of the same from the rights of a former owner. The latter in terms of its concept always refers to the former.

Original acquisition is of three forms: *absolute, extinctive,* and *accessory* acquisition.

1. *Absolute* acquisition is that in which, beginning entirely anew, an ownerless object is first brought into private ownership. Landed property by its nature – it being a continuum and it being the basis of communal satisfaction – is based as a rule on *distribution by the community – assignation, enfeoffment,* etc. Movables, however, by their nature – in which such considerations do not apply – are

based on *individual appropriation* in accordance with the principle of freedom, which is valid for property*.[41]

This consists above all in gaining physical power over the object – *occupation*. It answers to the nature of property as the right of corporeal control over an object that self-effected physical control form both its foundation and initial aspect, that through it the object be considered as shackled to the legal sphere of the person. This is because it de facto brings about **<78>** the condition which is elevated through law to the character of duration (Book II [*Principles of Law*], §. 5), which is property.[42] Mere will therefore is not enough for appropriation [Aneignung], nor is the objective identifiability of the same, since it does not bring about this condition; it is the achievement of the deed, the finished taking of possession, which does so. Whether then the mere *act* of *seizure* is sufficient or whether *continued* holding [Innehabung] and use is required (usucapion), in order for the thing to be viewed as being subjected to our physical power, is purely a positive establishment.[43] That the thing must be own- **<79>** erless is

[41]Now not even *fallow farmland* [Lehden] can be occupied by individuals.

[42] The ethical effect of law is therefore none other than the conferring of the permanence corresponding to spiritual being, by means of the will and mutual recognition, to relations which man is incapable physically of attaining. One might also apply Kant's viewpoint here, that time and empirical conditions must be mentally abstracted away, more properly, that the human will be elevated over it, be master of it.

[43]For example, in what degree is it possible to occupy landed property in the case of its not being publicly assigned? I can traverse unending amounts of land and put up signs, of which I perhaps cannot cultivate or truly manage the hundredth part. That the act of taking possession must protect me from ejection [Dejektion] stands to reason but it is not yet property. On the other hand, shall the mere act of seizure be sufficient for me to be able to demand surrender [daß ich vindiciren könne] when through accident another and then a third party [ein Anderer und ein Dritter] come into possession, for me to acquire an enduring and absolutely actionable [unbedingt verfolgbares] right – shall not much more an enduring use (**usucapio** of one year or such like) be required through which the material thing is assimilated to my condition, in a certain sense gradually permeated by the atmosphere of my right [meines Rechts], the true basis of my personal existence? This appears to be the oldest meaning of **usucapio** in the **res mancipi**, that

based in the concept of taking possession as a form of absolute acquisition – its entire meaning refers to this situation. Ownerlessness is however for that reason only a precondition, not the ground of acquisition. Given the equal possibility of such appropriation for all, the taking of possession is ever a form of *priority*, and therefore the acquisition of property through the taking of possession is based on a dual ground: the recognition of the person and his act, which is the principle of all priority (§. 4), and the purpose of the institution of property, by virtue of which it not only lends mere preference in factual conditions but gives an enduring right.

Beyond taking of possession, the appropriation of movables consists further in *manufacture* (**specificatio**). The self-production of an object is by eternal law the truest and most absolute ground of property. Although manufacture is not production in the fullest sense, since it presupposes a material, it is nevertheless so in relation to the object [Sache] in this shape or form, to this sort [Species]. Where therefore the earlier shape cannot be recovered, or beyond that where the form is the essential thing,[44] manufacture can rightly hold as the production of a new thing the property of which is due the maker, and the former thing, and therefore likewise the property in it held by another, as having expired. For this reason, manufacture is not yet extinctive acquisition since the original prop-

---

from the beginning it could come to be considered strict property, with the effect of vindication, not through occupation but only through continued possession. The Germanic seizure of three days is based on the same idea while also on the idea of publicness [Oeffentlichkeit], the relationship to the whole, that the independent right is acquired at the conveyance only after a year and a day. Could this not at least be evidence that no legal decision can be derived immediately from law-ideas ("natural law"), since the natural-law theory precisely here tends to present the matter in such a manner that the Roman **rei vindicatio** follows imperatively from the seizure of an abandoned thing according to a command of reason.

[44]The Roman criterion, whether the thing can be put back in its former shape, is too external to be adequate in itself; for example, a great sculptor having molded a statue using someone else's clay would have to leave it to the owner of the clay. The consideration as to whether the main value consists in the form had naturally still to arise, analogous to the maxim regarding accession.

erty is not abrogated as such and directly (legally) but only directly (factually) through the expiration of the thing.

2. Extinctive *acquisition* is that which, in relation to already existing property of another, proceeds not as its continu- <80> ation but its abrogation. It consists in *adverse possession* (usucapion in its contemporary meaning). Just as when possession is obtained it has the power to grant property in an ownerless thing, so with its continuation, in accordance with the principle of prescription (Book II [*Principles of Law*], §. 38), does it have the power to liquidate existing property; but only – in accordance to the ethical principle of legislation – when possession is *reasonable*, be it merely inner reasonable awareness (**bona fides**) which is required, be it an outward occurrence justifying it (**justa causa**), and regardless of whether reasonable awareness (lack of awareness of ownership on the part of another) is required only at the moment of gaining possession or more strictly until the period of adverse possession ends.

3. *Accessory* acquisition is the acquisition of a thing through its connection with another with which we already have a legal relation, be it by way of *outward accrual* (**accessio**, **alluvio**, etc.) or inward *organic generation* (acquisition of fruits). Here it is the *connection* to the primary thing, and our legal relation to it, upon which the acquisition is grounded, according to various considerations depending on the two main forms.[45]

Occupation is to be considered the primeval origin of all property at most to the degree that the people from whom the allocation of landed property proceeds, itself occupied that land.[46] But the property of individuals had its initial origin pre- <81> dominantly in the distribution by the community, in that the

---

[45]In the former case, the owner of the primary thing [Hauptsache] is to acquire the accessory thing [Nebensache] by reason of inseparability. In the latter case, the separation of the accessory thing (fruit) from the primary thing is what nature is after, and therefore here it is precisely someone other than the owner of the primary thing (**bona fide** possessor, beneficiary) who acquires, albeit by virtue of his relation to the owner.

[46]This is only occupation vis-à-vis other peoples. By contrast, that the conquered Samnitic land fell to the Roman state and not to the conquering soldiers, and that English lands fell to King William I and not to the barons who fought with him, is not based on the principle of occupation but on the relation between state or sovereign and individual.

acquisition of land, this cornerstone of all possession, as a rule proceeds from it. The subjective isolating natural law theory (even Hegel) ignores this and constructs all property upon the foundation of self-appropriation by individuals, contrary to history as well as to the idea. In general, occupation, regardless of the significant place it takes in legal philosophy due to its absolute origin, nevertheless in real life is an extremely rare and furthermore usually impure application; for the occupation of game, of fish, etc., usually depends on preconditions (authorization for hunting, fishing, etc.). The connectedness with which peoples and generations expand across the world of things, and in which in fact the spiritual existence of the human race consists, precisely entails that there was no room for such an absolute isolated act. Now that society has grown old, property as a rule is based on bequeathal, and where it is to arise in already existing things (not in those which first must be manufactured), it does so not through absolute beginning but through the liquidation of previous property, through usucapion. According to true doctrine, property must in the final analysis be derived from authority, not from acting on one's own [Eigenmacht] (§. 26) and must be construed in its continuity, by which it passes through the generations as a general condition of property*, not as an isolated, newly initiated acquisition of individuals.

§. 44. Derivative Acquisition

Derivative acquisition, as derivation from the rights of a former owner, has the character of being conditioned by the property of predecessors. It is based either on higher personal bonds to them – and thus is the consequence of a representa-
<82> tion of their person, whether the first acquirer or the last possessor (e.g., succession, **dos, arrogatio**) – or on the act of conveyance of the object in question.

The requirement of taking possession is not essential to derivative acquisition in the way in which it is for initial appropriation. In fact, with acquisition through representation it would be positively unnatural, in that here the right, by virtue of solidarity with the predecessor, is continued *as one's own*. But even with acquisition through conveyance it is not absolutely necessary, because one acquires power over the thing by means of the will of the other person. So, for example, according to the French law code property in movable things is acquired through mere contract; this makes it impossible for it to be sold dishonestly to a third party prior to realized physical transfer [erfolgter Tradition].

Roman law, by contrast, here too requires *physical transfer*. Herein is contained an extremely pointed expression of the inner significance of property, to wit, that lawful power over a thing can be initiated in no other way than through acquisition of the physical thing. For this it provides yet a great advantage. Namely, it is appropriate to properly appointed legislation that the moment of transfer of property be precisely designated, and this cannot more appropriately occur than through conveyance. With immovable things, either public recognition of conveyance or at least public pronouncement of the same is customarily required in the public interest. Here public registration and the like designates the transfer, making corporeal delivery a superfluous requirement.

Chapter 5: Possession

§. 45. The Nature of Possession

<83> The factual situation of power over the thing, exercised with the intention of ownership but without property having been established, does not extend any right to the thing; nevertheless, like property it serves the general purpose of property*: human satisfaction through things by means of free power over them (by means of their subjection to the will). For that reason it is appropriate that legal protection be granted it, only of another sort than property, namely not security in the *thing itself* and therefore against anyone who *withholds the thing*, but only security of the *factual situation*, and thus only against those who *abrogate this situation* (through their *positive act)*. This is our institution of *possession.* Its intention is not to protect the person against violence but to *conserve the factual situation towards things.*

With its violation, possession therefore vouchsafes not mere claims for compensation (**actio injuriarum**) but a claim to non-interference with or return of the thing. But it secures these only against those acts the form and manner of which endanger the *security of the factual situation* towards the thing,[47] namely, against forcible or clandestine <84> seizure or the attempt thereto. These are the specific violations of possession.[48] Possession therefore is only secured against *certain forms* of damage, namely those directly, physically caused by another (this alone is the disturbance of the factual situation), and thus always under the premise of a *positive* (active) injury (tort) on the other side (Book II [*Principles*

---

[47]This is what characterizes those actions as torts. Although their character as tort presupposes that they injure the *person* – not, as Puchta explained it, that the person is bodily harmed (this only being true in the case of forcible seizure), but that the will of the person to have the thing is violated – that character itself consists in the violation of the *factual situation towards the thing* acquired by the person. The former is the general basis of private tort, which therefore is also found in every other form of it, while the latter is the specific and positive basis for which reason they are torts.

[48]That the withholding of **precarium** in Roman law falls under the viewpoint of violation of possession rather than violation of contract is of a purely positive character and had good historical grounds.

of Law], §. 49) and is only *indirectly* secured by means of a claim on this violator (**actio in personam**). For this reason it is by no means an in itself neutral fact, obtaining legal significance only as a natural precondition to injurious actions; instead, in accordance with the above, it contains its legal significance within itself and only for this reason do those actions count as injurious. Upon this basis, its existence (acquisition, loss) likewise is not merely a matter of factual assessment but through legislation is joined to juristic criteria.

The institution of possession is therefore a *provisional* or *subsidiary arrangement* of the same life relation the actual intended and definite arrangement of which is the institution of property, to wit, the relation of men to things; but just because of this, it is not an arrangement like property which takes the view of the *right to the thing*, but which takes the view of the *mutual actions* of men, that the one not intentionally injure the other in his factual situation.[49] **<85>**

§. 46. Possession First Recognized by Roman Law

The extension of protection to possession as a special institution alongside property is therefore characteristic of the Roman law; because where a legal system recognizes the right to the thing not pure and simple but with regard to the actions of all participating persons and the events between them (see above, §. 36), property and possession merge into each other. Thus, even the Germanic Gewehre in movable things is such a cross between property and possession in that in it, as in Roman possession, legal help is only vouchsafed against positive unlawful privation (not against every form of withholding) of the thing, but even against the third-party possessor, as with Roman property. By contrast, in Roman law, in which property is recognized as the unconditional right to the thing, a second sphere is set apart for the relation to things according to that viewpoint.

---

[49] Compare above, §. 36. By the way, by no means does this explain the condition of the possessor (in subjective relation) to be provisional property (the possessory interdicts as provisional vindications), although the institution of possession (objectively as legislative arrangement) contains a provisional regulation for the same situation, the definitive regulation of which is property. Even less so, of course, is possession then a *presumptive* property. Legislation protects the factual situation not because it has the presumption of the law in its favor, but because as factual situation it merits conservation.

In Roman law, the protection of possession, at least in the more ancient period, also had a generically different character from that of property. The latter is based on recognition of unconditional subjective entitlement, the former, by contrast, on public order (by no means against violence and disturbance of the public peace, but for the maintenance of the factual situation to things as such), thus especially with the **ager publicus**, to which private entitlement was unthinkable. In the former case, the power of the ruling authorities serves private claims as superior force, so to speak; in the latter, the private claim first springs from the ruling authority.[50] **<86>**

§. 47. The Relation of Possession to Property

If the inner purpose of the protection of possession is as described – a provisional, subsidiary arrangement of the relation to things, the definitive and true arrangement of which is property – then possession must remain in a *constant relation to property*. Possession is to arrange these relations according to those factual considerations only in the case where legal considerations are lacking, and therefore must give way where such arise. Roman law (and even more, Roman theory) does not accord this relation its rightful importance.[51] It allows possession and property to run alongside each other without connection, in that, without regard for the institution's deeper origin and goal, it treats the claim to restitution on account of forcible or clandestine seizure merely as an

---

[50] As with all interdicts, the ones dealing with possession are based on the authority of the praetor: an accusation is made not because of the violation of a right but because something has been done contrary to the command of the praetor. The character of all **judicia imperio continentia**, to which they also belong, is no other than that their principle is the power of the ruling authorities [obrigkeitliche Gewalt] and not, as with the **judicia legitima**, recognized entitlement. Cf. my *Ancient Roman Law of Accusation* ["älteres römisches Klagenrecht"].

The protection of possession later was elevated [erstarkt] to a full-fledged private-legal institution. For this reason in our legal system protective measures regarding the factual situation in things have been added to the provisories [Provisorien – temporary rulings] which, as originally with **possessio**, are founded not on the right of the party but on the regard for and solicitude of the judge.

[51] **Nihil commune habet proprietas cum possessione** [property has nothing in common with possession], l. 12 §. 1 de adqu. vel amitt. poss. (41.2).

independent **obligatio ex delicto**, by which the right to the thing is not even taken into account. Only in one respect did the deeper motive of the matter assert itself in Roman law: the **interd. ret. poss.** was used as preparation in the property suit to establish the role of the defendant. <87>

By contrast, German procedural practice, partially derived from the canon law, reconstituted this connection. This is expressed in particular in:

1. Above all, that the incontrovertible defense [(liquide) Einrede] of property is sustained against the possessory action (interdict) [gegen die Besitzklage (Interdikt) Statt hat];

2. That **possessorium** and **petitorium** are treated not as procedures concerning entirely different things, the former a delictual obligation, the latter concerning property, but as procedures aiming at one final goal, thus that cumulation of the two takes place;

3. That the entire institution is extended to legal relations of the character of real rights other than property and in fact partly to those concerning which a similar formal injury as a rule virtually never occurs, but the purpose of which merely is the conservation of a provisional situation until the definitive legal inquiry.[52]

These and similar determinations are therefore not to be considered as disfigurements and misunderstandings of the Roman law but rather as natural advances and improvements of it. In no way is the Roman, independent development of both institutions – property in its thing-oriented, absolute character, possession in its only indirect protection by means of the **obligatio ex delicto** – thereby to be forfeited, but only finally reoriented to their common higher goal. The Roman <88> shape of the institution, first clarified by Savigny, and its formation in German practice up until that point are entirely divergent in terms of technical structure, the former based upon the opposition of property and delictual obligation, the latter on the opposition between **definitivum** and **provi-**

[52]One could also count among these, that in accordance with practice a better possession can be asserted to be in **possessorium**, i.e., not in consideration of a better possession from formal consideration of disturbance (**vi clam**, etc.) but from material grounds ("**possessor antiquior et titulata**"), like the leading procedurists (Bayer, Linde et al.) still presume; but this practice, as Savigny has shown, rests merely on a misunderstanding of canon law and should instead be abandoned.

sorium. Our legal-philosophical principle – the purpose (τέλος) of possession – demands that they nevertheless be united in such a manner that the motivating factor and the goal of this practice remain preserved, and the entire Roman technical apparatus be consciously inserted as medium, as the manner of achieving that goal, under the cited modifications which this goal entails.

§. 48. The Place of Possession in the Legal System

When classified according to the true systematic viewpoint, to wit, as *legal institution,* possession has its *position in the system* undoubtedly among *real rights.* Its purpose is the ordering of the relation to the thing. Should one however systematize in terms of that subordinate viewpoint of rights and the objects of those rights, then possession has no place in that system, or rather that classification, since it is no right to an object. For "right" in the sense of our legal system involves an unconditional protection, that is, one independent of the continuity of a factual condition, and "object of right" is accordingly an object (thing, performance) which is to be the entitled's pure and simple, all of which simply does not hold true for possession. For this reason, possession here only comes into consideration as factual precondition for **obligationes ex delicto** (interdicts).[53] **<89>**

§. 49. Theories of Possession: Savigny, Thibaut, Gans, Puchta

Savigny clarified the obscurity over this doctrine which had reigned until he came along, and his "Law of Possession" is the model of a juristic monograph. The significance of possession originates in the fact that it is a factual relation which corresponds to property as legal relation, it is a protection against formal (i.e., positive) unlawful acts, it is therefore a juristically relevant and protected fact, not a right, etc.; these enlightening viewpoints were emphasized by him, and all of us therefore stand upon the foundation he laid. That Savigny treated

[53] Nor can I agree with Puchta regarding this doctrine from a systematic viewpoint. To wit, he describes possession as a "right to one's own will" or a "right to one's own person." The "rights to one's own person" in that case would be twofold: 1) the right of personality, 2) the right of possession. But possession, in that it has an *external object* and presumes an *act of acquisition*, cannot possibly hold as a mere right to one's own will or to one's own person and form a class together with honor and the like. Such would only be the general capacity to possess, not possession of a specific thing.

possession merely as the precondition for the **obligationes ex delicto** and not as an independent legal institution is the standpoint of the Roman law itself, which to elucidate faithfully in its own coherence was his task. The entire juristic formation of the Roman law of possession is thereby given, in classical, irreproachable completion. On the other hand, I cannot so unconditionally fall in with Savigny regarding the final motive of this formation. For the innermost relation of possession, that it is the same relation to the thing factually as property is legally, which precisely Savigny first clarified – he puts it at the pinnacle of his treatment only straightaway to give it up, in that he grants it no significance in itself but allows it to arise merely from the necessarily accompanying injury of the person. He thereby makes the inviolability of the person himself rather than the inviolability of his position with regard to the thing to be the foundation of the institution of possession. In spite of this, in his course on civil law Savigny, with sure legal-philo- **<90>** sophical insight, assigned possession its proper systematic position among real rights.

Thibaut rightly asserts that the maintenance of the provisional situation is the core of entire institution of possession, and that accordingly possession does not first gain significance through the interdict but vice versa, the latter only exists for the sake of the former. But firstly Thibaut hereby does not distinguish between the legislative or law-constructive motive and the juristic (technical) principle, and therefore rejects Savigny's unassailable disclosure of that principle; furthermore, Thibaut conceives the former, true motive in an unsuitable generality as protection of the provisional situation in general, the exercise of rights in general, without regard for the entirely specific nature of factual power over things (the analogy to property), and thus arrives at his misconceived systematic classification of possession within the General Part. From this so very generally conceived motive, nothing indeed can be gained for possession than what in similar manner holds for the provisionally existing marital status, for the defendant against a claim, etc., and precisely the characteristic effects of possession remain for him, as he himself admits, without explanation as something incidental, something positive.

It is exactly the truth of the Savignian doctrine which Gans combats, in that he asserts that possession is no less than "a decisive right,"[54] certainly unlawful

---

[54] Gans, *Foundation of Possession* [Grundlage des Besitzes], p. 33.

with respect to property, but this relativity holds true for all rights. Gans finds support for this assertion in the face of the undeniable factual nature of possession in the fact that every right is based on a fact, thus possession, in that it also enjoys legal protection, of necessity is **<91>** of the same nature as all other rights.[55] This however is an obvious confusion of the fact as being a transitory versus an immanent cause of rights. Every right requires a fact for its *origin*, e.g., property requires delivery, usucapion, etc., but once this has occurred, the right continues its own independent existence, even when the fact ceases. By contrast, possession requires the fact for its *continuance* as well; should the fact cease, so would its protection. From this viewpoint, it is not a right but merely a legally protected factual situation. Just for this reason, possession is likewise not merely lesser in terms of power or degree than property, not even a relative property ("inchoate property"); this would be appropriate to the **bonae fidei possessio**, but not to **possessio**, it rather being something entirely different in character. Just as untenable as this foundation of Gans's argumentation – that all rights are based upon a fact in the same way as possession – is the other foundation, that all rights stand in a relation of relativity one to another, like possession and property: "the significance of rights is always to be understood only in the relationship, not absolutely."[56] "In the way possession is unlawful against property, so is property against contract, contract against family, family against the state, the state against history." For the latter is neither true, nor does it apply to the relation between possession and property. Instead, property, contract, family, state are pure independent spheres, of which one cannot say that the one must yield to the other, must be "unlawful" against it, e.g., the family is just as holy as the state, and the state cannot dissolve family ties, etc.; by contrast, against property juristic possession is unlawful and void pure and simple. Beyond this, the **<92>** author's argumentation is moved by the truth that possession is an institution aimed at the relation to the thing in the same way as property, that "the will of the person, where it expresses itself in things, is a right," and thus the grounding of possession must be a direct and not an indirect one; but that is something

---

[55] "All legal concepts are however facts [Fakta]: I possess, have property, marry, inherit. These are facts, but there is a relation in them which one cannot deny the name of legal."

[56] *ibid.*, p. 38.

entirely different from "inchoate property" in the sense in which he applies it. Moreover, the practical goal of this polemic cannot be discerned.

Puchta's concept that possession *"derives"* its legal nature from the *"right of personality"* (i.e., that each ouster injures the will of the person) discloses an essential aspect of the legal-philosophical rationale of possession, although it does not exhaust it. Not only possession but no less property stems from the rights of personality, the recognition of the will, in the manner of the natural law teachers who actually deduce them solely from this. No less so contract. But the protection of possession, just as that of property, does not yet have its complete rationale and its specific formation in these rights of personality. It is not the ungrounded will of the person in and of itself which the law is to protect and has the vocation to protect, but the advantage gained from others under the favor of circumstances, the factual position with respect to the thing. That will is only the necessary precondition for this, which is no less the case for property, for the acquisition of the inheritance, etc. The will and its importance – as Puchta stresses – is the one side of the law-constructing principle, the other however is the significance of life relations in which the will is operative (compare §§. 1, 29, 56), in this case the situations towards things.

Therefore Savigny finds the basis of the protection of possession in the inviolability of the *body* of the person, Puchta in the inviolability of the *will*, I by contrast directly in the invio- **<93>** lability of their *factually existing relations to the thing.* Just as adverse possession and the gradual legitimacy of usurped thrones have one and the same principle (Savigny), just so do the protection of juristic possession and the esteem for de facto governments have one and the same principle, and if the latter did not exist, the former could not either. Juristic possession serves the same purpose (satisfaction through things) in unentitled fashion that property serves in entitled fashion; de facto government serves the same purpose (maintenance of public order) in unentitled fashion that legitimate governments serve in entitled fashion. In both cases, although the *subjects* have no title, the *objective relation* (the use of things, the maintenance of order) is justified and is something that should exist. Therefore subjects without title are protected or respected, as the case may be, as long as they are not confronted with an entitled subject.

Chapter 6: Obligation and Contract

§. 50. Personal Rights: Property in the Acts of Others

<95> Performances [Leistungen] by other people serve the needs of our existence just as much as does the possession of things, and the activity of personality in freely giving shape to the way of life, which requires property in things, therefore also requires the same power of free disposal and the same enduring secure right over that other means of existence. This enduring secure right is *obligation* (**obligatio**) in contradistinction to merely factual, momentary performance (**datio**). Obligation serves a dual purpose, that of meeting needs for which things are not appropriate (services, works), but beyond that, securing things for the future by means of the human will. The significance of obligation is not so much to make possible services or the communication of things – this can be achieved by mere factual performance – but instead to secure the future, partly by making possible a present performance or communication (**commodatum**, **mutuum**) without damage and hazard, and partly through which the future possession of an object is secured in a manner often not afforded even by continuous possession. For example, when I deposit an object or lend an amount, this might well secure the thing much better than if I held onto it. Herein lies an intellectualization of property*.

Obligation consequently is one's right to another's performance bearing some property* value, be it delivery of an ob- **<96>** ject, be it pure act. It is of a totally different character than the true rights of the person (family, class, corporation rights etc.), which have as their object dependence or commitment among the persons themselves, with an ethical and not merely pecuniary significance. Performance of the most intellectual [geistigsten] kind can also be the object of obligation (for example tutelage, education, artistic performance), albeit only to the degree that they permit a wage and money-equivalent in accordance with general estimation and practice. That which cannot in any way be considered an acquisition and something with money value (for example to be elected mayor, to be taken on as confessor) cannot be an object of obligation.

Because the individual performance of a person cannot be separated from his entire personality, an overriding question facing law and justice is the relation between the enforceability of the former and the freedom of the latter.

Purely personal actions (such as services) cannot be made perpetual objects of obligation because they then become a personal dependence of the person. Purely personal actions furthermore cannot be coerced to the degree that they alter the total personal position in life of the obligee (e.g., a singer having to keep an engagement after having decided to give up singing as a career). The Romans therefore only handed down sentences in terms of general money value even for obligations entailing the provision of specific objects. Lastly, the person of the debtor should not be treated as an object of collateral for a performance of a pecuniary sort, as in the older Roman law, which allowed for the sale or the cutting into pieces of the debtor. *Imprisonment for debt* is not justified on the ground that the person himself is collateral for the performance, but on the ground that imprisonment in general is the means of the ruling authority to hold people to the fulfillment of their **<97>** obligations, both public and private. Neither therefore does it rest on contract, as something which cannot take place due to the inalienable right of freedom, but on protection by the ruling authority. Therefore the abolition of imprisonment for debt is an injustice against the creditor, the denial of government help, and, because it destroys personal credit, an injustice against all those in need of credit. However, this must have regulation and limits – eternal imprisonment for failure of performance to the creditor is unjustified because the person himself is not likewise a subsidiary object of obligation. By contrast, the property* of the debtor stands unconditionally as guarantee for these performances of pecuniary value.

§. 51. The Forms of Obligation

The many specific kinds [Species] of obligation derive from the multiplicity of needs of reciprocal grant or regarding the mutual assurance of future provision, as for example the transfer of objects as property or for use, hire of services, exchange, etc. They are the ways developed in common life by which one person can be made liable to another. But in order for these obligations to exist between specific persons there must be a specific ground, an event (**causa**) between them. In every such event, both the persons of creditor and debtor are designated[57]

[57]The **actiones quod met. caus., ad exhib., de glande legenda**, actions of injury [Noxalklagen] therefore are not true **obligationes** but pure **actiones**, the **debitor** not being designated once and for all through the *event* but determined and fixed only through

and the content of **<98>** the obligation more closely specified. It is then likewise characteristic that the nature of the obligation, the principles of its treatment, are determined by the grounds of its origin (obligations of contract, tort, alimony, legacy); property on the other hand is always the same regardless of its origin, whether it be through occupation, usucapion or whatever.

§. 52. Origin and Goals of Obligations

All obligations have the goal of establishing a communication of property* *either originally, or as a substitute* for previously caused damages, the former in consequence of actions and events which in the view of the parties or in accordance with their own nature have as their purpose the foundation of a legal relation (*transaction* [Geschäft] in the widest sense), the latter in consequence of a *debt* owed by the obligee. Accordingly, one may distinguish between two main forms of obligation, *transaction* obligations and *tort* obligations, which then are subject to a generically different treatment.[58]

The origin of obligations, which, in accordance with the above, likewise determines the treatment of the same and thus its classification, is however more specifically the following. In accordance with the general dual principle of all legal origin (Book II [*Principles of Law*], §. 37), this is based partly on the *freedom of the parties involved*, partly on the *given specific relations* among them. The former has the priority, because the sphere of property* is characterized by freedom. Obligations arise from freedom either **<99>** through contract or injury, the former obligating fulfillment, the latter damages (Book II [*Principles of Law*], §. 49). The given relations which in accordance with the purpose of life conditions generate an obligation are manifold in accordance with the nature of these relations, for which reason the Romans summarized them under the

---

the **lit. cont.** The extra-judicial refusal of restitution therefore does not here justify a substitute action, grounds no **mora**, etc., there are only **actiones** and not **obligationes**. Furthermore, the determinate person of creditor belongs to the essence of an obligation. The **cessio actionum** is an expansion, not the abolition of this principle. An exception to this is our obligations au porteur, which however is an institution of public-legal character.

[58] The claim for damages arising from a contract is a transaction obligation; it is not meant to restore damages caused but to fulfill that which was promised of an original distribution, its value or interest, as the case may be.

designation "**ex variis causarum figuris**" [from a variety of reasons]. Nevertheless, these main classes may be distinguished among them:

1. Some arise from the purpose of property* transactions, similar to contractual obligations. The need to secure a return or substitute through agreement also creates an obligation immediately, apart from agreement, in cases in which such is actually not possible or is customarily omitted due to prevailing opinion and expectation. Here belong most of the Roman law's "quasi-contracts," e.g., **negotiorum gestio**, claims for restitution [Kondiktionen], etc.[59]

2. Some arise in the purpose of other institutions, namely familial and successional relations, in order to realize claims arising from these, as for example endowment, alimentary obligations, **actio tutelae**, legacy, etc.

3. Some are merely for the purpose of protecting other rights, namely property rights, and thus are more **actiones** than **obligationes**, for example **ad exhibidendum, damni infecti cautio, de glande legenda, de arbor. caedendis**, etc. <100>

§. 53. Obligation not Limited to Contract

The most significant ground of origin of obligations, derived purely from the purpose of property* transactions, is *contract*.

Misled by this, legal philosophers, in particular Kant and Hegel, viewed contract rather than obligation as the other aspect of property* over against property, in contradiction both to legal practice and true relations. Certainly, contract is the form of origin of obligation κατ᾽ ἐξοχήν [par excellence], because origin through contract has its root purely in the purpose of property* transactions, and thus in obligation itself; nevertheless, it is not the only ground of its origin. Obligation is not merely to serve voluntary property* transactions but also the fulfillment of familial bonds, successional relations, settlement of property claims and the like, and, what is more decisive, contract in turn is not restricted to obligations but also forms the basis of other legal bonds. It is only the abstraction by which the bare relationship of will is accentuated, that the one will is bound to the other, without consideration of the object (whether for a performance of pecuniary value, for a future marriage, for a relationship of

[59]In similar manner, the duty to provide compensation is sometimes, out of equity for that which was damaged, extended to such to which, strictly speaking, violation ought not be imputed – "quasidelict," which then are treated analogously to tort obligations.

protection such as fealty, for a goal respecting the law of nations, etc.) from which stems such a complete identification of contract with obligation.

§. 54. The Nature of Contract

Contract is a mutual stated agreement among specific persons regarding a legal relationship to be founded amongst themselves.

Contract in the broadest sense is of *two different forms.* It is either a mere means of founding legal relations which immediately afterward separate from contract to continue an existence <101> in accordance with their own requirements and laws, for example marriage, **pactum hypothecae**, physical delivery, ratification of the state constitution. Or it contains the legal relation in itself and continues to be the latter's cause and source (substance), so that complete fulfillment continuously proceeds only in pursuance of the agreement and according to the standard it sets. To this pertain above all contracts of obligation [Forderungsverträge], but not these alone: others do as well, for example, in some respects engagement to be married, then contracts in the law of nations (e.g., alliance). For example, spouses require of each other faithfulness to vows, support, shared lifestyle, not because of agreement made in concluding the marriage but because of marriage itself; the property owner does not lay claim to an object because of physical delivery but because it is his property; on the other hand, the buyer, the renter, the principal lodges a claim because of a contract and in accordance with it.[60] In the former case contract is the transitory cause, in the latter case the immanent cause. The former are contractual *acts*, the latter contractual *relations*, that is to say, the former arise through contract (agreement) without themselves being contracts.[61]

---

[60] In this manner, the North American opposition understood the Union to be a treaty and thus dissoluble; but the principle was pushed through that although the foundation of the Union was a treaty, currently the Union is no treaty but rather a fundamental determinant [Grundbestimmung] of the North American state constitution.

[61] So is the divergence dispelled between Hegel, *Natural Law* [Naturr. – a.k.a. *Philosophy of Law*], §. 75, and Savigny, *Pand.* [a.k.a. *System of Modern Roman Law*], Book III, p. 307, concerning whether marriage is a contract. The determinations regarding consensus (error, condition) for which reason Savigny aims to establish the quality of contract certainly have their application in the *solemnization* of the marriage, which is a

<102> In the former class, the act of agreement and fulfillment coincide in a single moment; for example, marriage is likewise fulfilled through consent, because further fulfillments, as already noted, are based not on consent but in marriage itself, just as the lien is already extended with the closing of the **pactum hypothecae**. By contrast, in the latter class future fulfillment, which can be required only through contract, is what is in view; this brings up the question regarding legal obligation to fulfillment following a change of will in the meantime – the weightiest problem faced by early "natural law."

§. 55. Contract as the Expression of Freedom and Faithfulness

Freedom lies in the *essence of the person*, providing on the one hand the possibility of devotion, disposal, on the other enlargement; therefore *immutability* lies also in that essence, in accordance with which the disposal now willed is also willed in all its consequences, taking them into account with the same certainty as with something already present. From this is derived the possibility not only of immediate grant (**datio**) but for agreement in a bond of will in accordance with which it is granted in future. This agreement is *contract*, that is, promise and acceptance as one element, and the immutability through which the arisen confidence (faith) in the future is fulfilled is *faithfulness* [Treue] (**fides**), that original characteristic of personality. Contract is based on freedom and faithfulness, but *its binding character is faithfulness.*[62] Faithfulness is the ethical **<103>** idea of all contractual bonds, both legal and moral.

---

contractual act, but with regard to marriage itself, which is no contract, they have this only in restricted measure.

[62]Should one, as do most natural-law teachers since Kant, e.g. Gros (*Textbook of Natural Law* [Lehrbuch des Naturrechts]), derive the obligatory nature of contract [Vertrag] simply from freedom ("the possibility of any causality"), then one can deduce the possibility of present conveyance and performance but not future commitment. The latter lies not in freedom but in immutability and faithfulness, as Kant himself rightly recognizes. At any rate, however, *freedom* in its true significance and *faithfulness* are concepts which mutually postulate each other, namely the divergent and indissoluble attributes of personality. Therefore it is *not freedom but personality* from which *contracts* are to be deduced. The claim that faithfulness is a mere moral and not legal concept is one of those fundamental errors of abstract natural law, denuding law of ethical ideas (cf. Book II [*Principles of Law*], §. 6).

Contract is therefore the means by which free beings by their wills and this certain immutability establish a bond between themselves that in itself and in terms of necessity would not otherwise exist between them. This contractual bond is essentially different from the bond of love: its commitment does not arise through one's making the well-being of another a goal of his own, but simply through the immutability of one's own will, the demonstration of the arisen faith. The former is a giving up of separate purposes and interests, the persons themselves becoming as one; the latter premises the preservation of the complete separation of purposes and interests, and exists because of this separate existence.

§. 56. Contract More than Mere Mutual Willingness

When in this manner contract fully freely and absolutely originally establishes a bond of obligation for those engaging in it, it still requires for this a basis in the makeup of the bond whereby it of itself and in general serves a higher order and necessity. This is therefore the point at which merely moral contracts diverge from those that are legally binding. For a contract to be binding only morally, it should serve an ethical, in which case a rational goal. Neither the unethical nor the purposeless contract has any moral obligation. For a contract to be fully binding legally, it must serve a legal goal, <104> that is, its content must have a relation that forms a necessary component of common life and thus the legal order, for example marriage, obligation in its various types, purchase, exchange, rent. The union of wills is therefore certainly the actual binding factor (by virtue of faithfulness) but even so it is only binding under the precondition of that content. Therefore, obligations in particular are by no means the mere product of human freedom and union of wills; they are already delineated spheres in the order of common life, the union of wills being only the means for particular persons to engage in these, albeit – because, being property* relations, they belong to the sphere of freedom – certainly also determining them more precisely in terms of content. The purpose of property* transactions require that such exist and requires that they exist only in accordance with the will of the parties involved; for this reason contract is the means for establishing them, and vice versa, the contract having them as content is legally binding. That the union of wills alone does not establish legal obligation is confirmed hereby, that a contract which does not have such a relation as its object is likewise not legally binding,[63] and inversely, obligations may also arise apart from contract simply in accordance with the need of property* transactions when persons are indicated for them in some other fashion, e.g. **condictio indebiti, negot. gestio.**

Accordingly the binding force of contract, in accordance with the idea of private law as a whole (see above, §. 1), is based on two aspects: the essence of the person (freedom and faithfulness) and the purpose (τέλος) of the bonds it is to establish. The former is the subjective and therefore also the formal aspect, the latter the objective aspect. Kant brought the **<105>** subjective aspect, freedom and faithfulness, into view.[64] Kant however did not express his entire philosophical viewpoint in a positive manner, as from the will, which, unchangeable in time, wills the same then as now, but in a negative manner, requiring the elimination of the interim and the act of fulfillment (the "empirical conditions"), and viewing that which is granted as "presently," that is, as timelessly acquired. But then the entire natural law theory, in accordance with its viewpoints, leaves completely out of consideration the objective aspect, the higher order of the institution in which contract intervenes, that it serves as means, which alone distinguishes the legally binding contract from the merely morally binding, entirely analogously to how in the case of property that theory only considers the power of the ("subjective") will and not the ("objective") purpose of the same unto satisfaction.[65] **<106>**

---

[63]For example, a teacher or artist convinces another who obtains a commission to refuse it with the promise that he too will refuse the next commission offered himself. This, in particular when no pecuniary interest is involved, is not a legally binding contract even though *the act* of agreement has all the criteria of a contract.

[64]*Doctrine of Law*, p. 100. He believes that he is deducing from freedom what in fact he deduces from faithfulness.

[65]The *canon law's* arrangement regarding contracts engaged *under oath* is based on an error similar to that of the natural-law theory. The canon law as well attached the power effectuating collective obligation only to the subjective elements – the *agreement of the parties*, here strengthened by the oath – which in actuality is likewise located in the objective elements – the *suitability* [Qualifikation] *of the transaction* – in that it of necessity must depend on them. Roman law, by contrast, had the proper principle that a shortcoming in the objective elements, which are the precondition of all effectiveness,

§. 57. Contracts are Classified According to Purpose

Obligations derived from contracts are distinguished into various classes in accordance with their *content*, the purpose (τέλος) they are to serve. Every other distinction, even that according to the viewpoint of unilaterality as opposed to reciprocity, is more or less externally formal. Accordingly, the following main classes manifest themselves as natural relations with similar legal consequences:

1. Contracts consisting in *unilateral performance:* stipulation of performances, forbearances, endowment and the like. They are the simplest affairs, they contain the least degree of obligation (no **culpa levis**); in fact, because they comprise pure forfeiture, the question arises as to whether they are meant to be serious and binding, and to what degree they are allowable.

2. Contracts consisting in the *surrender of a thing against its return:* **commodatum**, **precarium**, **depositum**, **mutuum** and all the Roman innominate contracts comprising the relinquishment of a thing (in **genere** or **specie**) against its future return. Here also belong contracts in which a thing is given on certain grounds or for certain goals, subject to return should the ground prove unfounded or the goal not be attained, and such an obligation is constituted – subject to conditions – by the surrender even when there is no contract, merely due to the inner requirement of the transaction (claims for restitution [Kondiktionen]).

In accordance with their nature these contracts and transactions are in a certain sense real contracts; they comprise the surrender of a thing, this constitutes them, prior to this the obligation cannot exist. The contract through which a **mutuum**, **depositum**, etc., is given differs completely and <107> concerns an entirely different commercial need; the commitment of the receiver to return is not derived from the **pactum de mutuo dando** but always follows solely from the **mutuum** itself, the surrender of money in prospect of its return.

Surrender also forms an essential component of the transaction when the object of the right is to receive back. For this reason it has the character of re-

---

cannot be rectified by the mere strengthening of the subjective elements contained in the oath.

ciprocity, usually the **actio contraria**,[66] although with the more secure commitment, thus granting of **culpa levis**, usually only on one side.

3. Contracts comprising the *exchange of performances and grants:* purchase, exchange, rent, and everything that takes place in the four forms (*do ut des,* etc. – for example insurance contracts), if the same thing is not to be returned otherwise.

These contracts are essentially reciprocal, commitment beginning simultaneously on both sides. In this case the question therefore arises firstly as to who is to begin the performance, then the **exceptio non adimpleti contractus**, and finally the consideration as to whether involuntary hindrance on the one side frees the other side from having to do his part – both sides gain here, since as a rule both practice **culpa levis.**

4. Contracts comprising a *business relation*: **mandatum** and **societas**, each in accordance with its various forms.

What is particular to these is that their content is not from the outset established by specific performances; instead it is interpersonal relations that do so, because often no preset performances are established as a specific object. And one entirely characteristic consideration arises in this case, the legal relation to *third parties,* in that the nature of a business relation entails <108> the one standing surety for another, the one acquiring for another.

The need to conduct business allows the obligation to arise even without an order – **negotiorum gestio.**

The requirement arising from common danger also founds a social relation (to save oneself by incurring losses [jettisoning cargo to avoid shipwreck], but then to share the damages equally) without contract – **lex Rhodia de jactu** (treated by the Romans, quite inappropriately, as a modification of lease).

5. *Contracts of chance* [Glücksvertrage]: games, gambling. The character of these is that no true need exists for them in commerce; the main question in their case therefore is to what degree they are obligatory at all.

6. Contracts that serve an already existing obligation, either to confirm, to secure, or to modify it – *accessory* contracts: **constitutum**, pledge, novation.

[66] That the **mutuum** forms an exception to this lies not so much in the kind of binding force as in the object, to wit, the abstract sum through which and to which no damage can occur.

These deal with the requisite of the preceding obligation and the relation to it of newly arising ones.[67]

§. 58. Kant's Classification

The Roman system of contract is based on the special requirements of their actionability in accordance with Roman law and therefore possesses no general truth, and in particular is totally inappropriate for our <109> current situation. Kant[68] substituted for this a philosophical system in which contracts are either:

1. *Endowment* contracts (under which the interest-free loan, the **commodatum**, the **depositum**), or
2. *Exchange* contracts (purchase, exchange, authorization [Mandat], etc.), or finally
3. *Completion* [Vervollständigungs-] contracts (pledge, surety).

This system also found favor with Hegel.[69] In terms of both of their fundamental concepts this is certainly correct, but it has the fault that in its implementation it is erected merely on the form of performance (the **datio**) rather than on the form of obligation (the **obligatio**) and therefore is viewed in terms of the unilateral or bilateral character of the *benefit* rather than of the *legal bond;* and in general the diversity of obligation, both among the contracting parties and vis-à-vis third parties (for example, between purchase and partnership), which juristically is precisely of the most significance, does not take its proper place in this system.

---

[67]In this systematization of contracts, Pfordten (*Treatises from the Laws of the Pandects* [Abhandl. aus dem Pandektenrechte], p. 302) has already followed me regarding Roman law, and in greater detail. Proceeding from Pfordten, this system has gone over to Koch's account of the Prussian law of obligation.

[68]*Doctrine of Law*, p. 120.

[69]*Philosophy of Law*, §. 80.

PART THREE: THE FAMILY

Introduction

§. 59. The Nature of the Family

<110> The family serves the general natural purpose of *maintaining the race* [Gattung]. It fulfills this in such a way that man receives the satisfaction of the bonds of descent and love, and that the human race (or [bez.] the people) as a whole maintains the *unity of essence* which enables it to build a spiritual personal kingdom (Book I [*Philosophical Foundations*], §. 24). In consequence of the creatureliness of man and the material basis of his existence, this extension indeed takes place as mere procreation, hence man here participates in the general arrangement of nature: the race unfolds in both of the sexes, and procreation is linked to their physical complement and union. Solely by virtue of the personality of man, these relationships, which in the lower reaches of creation only form momentary passing acts, with him becoming enduring bonds permeating all of existence. The complement of the sexes becomes a bond of imperishable full personal devotion, becomes *marriage;* procreation becomes an enduring bond between parents and children, namely *upbringing,* this being the free communication of one's own human essence in accordance with its ethical spiritual side, just as procreation is the natural communication of the same in accordance with the mere natural side. As such, in this spiritual ethi- <112> cal character, they are the *institution of the family*. As the bond of descent and therefore essential unity, the family is however the sphere of love in eminent degree – because love (the self feeling and willing in another) everywhere has as its foundation the unity of substance – and is, because it founds the same unity of essence for the human race, the primeval source and archetype of love for neighbor.

Consequently the family is firstly a bond of corporeal unity (union of the sexes – descent), but this corporeal unity is the bearer of a higher spiritual unity, firstly of *love,* then of *vocation* on behalf of the purpose of the family, each with differing specific determinacy (married love, respect for elders, etc.) for the different members according to the nature of the organic bond.

§. 60. The Relations of Family

Family relations are therefore initially these two: marriage and the bond between parents and children, namely *authority of upbringing*. Joined to these, however, is *inheritance*, the succession in the property* of the deceased, as that which stems from the family, the continuation of personality and the love based on it being the foundation of all transmission of property*. Furthermore, artificial imitations of the bonds of the natural family also make their appearance, *guardianship* as a substitute for paternal protection and, as the case may be [bez.], paternal upbringing, and the *servant relation* as a substitute for the subsistence grounded in one's own family on the one hand, and as an extension of one of the goals of the family, namely external satisfaction through the provision of aid by the members, on the other. These also lack the sanctity of the family bond proper. **<113>**

§. 61. The Uniqueness of the Family Relation

The family stands out among all institutions of the legal order by its *moral character*,[70] while according to its entire being it is the inner union and devotion of specific persons. Simply through the moral motive of its members it already has an objective existence as an enduring organic bond prior to any law (that is, prior to any formation by the whole) and its legal formation likewise has the idea of personal devotion as its determining principle, in the same way that other institutions have the idea of freedom, justice and the like. *Love* is here *graphically displayed*. Under other circumstances love affects the requirement of individual acts; here it affects the construction, the shape of relations, for example the community of station [Standesgemeinschaft] of the spouses, the indissolubility of

[70]Even in morality [Moral] (subjective ethical behavior [subjektiven Sittlichkeit]), it distinguishes itself as an exceptionally sanctified relation. The basis for this is simply that the family has such a great significance in the natural economy; and then that the bond to which one owes existence, the primordial bond, is the innermost source of all that is ethical – *piety*. This is the supreme virtue, firstly piety towards the Creator, then towards our physical procreator. All ethical behavior is based on piety, and when separated from this it is no longer true ethical behavior.

the marriage bond.[71] Precisely because of this, however, the family is by no means a *mere* moral relation, with only *limited* influence on the law, but is in its entirety no less a legal institution in its own right; it is the task of the community to maintain it in its ethical shape, and its same ethical idea, the idea which determines the life of the members in it, that is, the moral requirement, also determines its shape in the common life, that is, its legal order; however, the latter does not realize this idea in its <114> full content but only in its most external (negative) contours (Book II [*Principles of Law*], §. 6).

§. 62. The Public Character of the Family

The family is the center of human existence, the bond of individual life and common life, as it constitutes the complete satisfaction of the individual while also being the means by which the race, and thus the community, civil and religious, arises, both corporeally and ethically-spiritually (through upbringing). For this reason state and church intervene here in a twofold manner: not merely, in accordance with the above, to maintain the *ethical form of the family* within the common condition, but also for the sake of their *own civil and ecclesiastical interests.* Thus for example the restrictions on marriage between close relations, the prohibition of arbitrary divorce, the duty to provide material support, are maintained because they are in accordance with marriage in its ethical requirement; but when the state links marriage to evidence of livelihood, to the approval of one's military commander, in that case it is not considerations of the ethical order of marriage that are at question but purely civil ones. The family therefore indeed is a private-legal institution and as such is based on the principle of individual freedom, but it is everywhere likewise permeated with standards of public interest (**publici juris**), that is, both good mores (**boni mores**) and civil and ecclesiastical considerations, which restrict individual freedom.

§. 63. The Characteristics of the Family

Accordingly, the characteristics of the law of the family are as follows:
<115>

---

[71] Therefore the objection to the indissolubility of marriage, that it is merely morally and not legally commanded by reason or Christ, is inadmissible; for in the case of the family it is precisely the moral principle which is simultaneously the objectively form-giving principle also determining law.

1. It contains not only rights but above all *an ethical and organic shape,* and thus order, necessity; for example, the impermissibility of certain marriages or divorce, the requirement of a shared life, etc.

2. The rights contained in it have the *person* as their object, that is, the inner, enduring dependence which fills life, and not things or isolated performances. Only in consequence of this personal dependence do material [sächliche] claims (**dos, peculium**) and individual benefits (alimony, endowment) arise.

3. These rights are as a rule *reciprocal,* not unilateral, in which the one party is the subject, the other is the object, as in the case of obligation.

4. These rights are always likewise *duties,* even in juridical perspective, and thus as a rule are not disposable or alienable even in the case of mutual consent.

5. The law of the family, because of the family's concrete [plastisch] organic character, not only entails the rights and duties of family members but also a *common legal position* in the state, for example station, legal domicile, etc. Accordingly, family bonds, marriage and filiation, must also be established in public general terms; they should not, like property* claims, apply against one opponent [Gegner] and not another, or in one country and not another.[72]

§. 64. The Shortcomings of the Natural-Law Concept

The earlier natural law theory, rendered incapable by its subjective standpoint of comprehending an organic relationship such as is exemplified in the family, degraded this institu- <116> tion to the lowest level. According to Kant, marriage is a contract for the mutual exclusive use of sexual functions, while with Fichte, unrestricted sexual intermingling can legally take place. With Gros, from the standpoint of the law of reason marriage can be engaged for a limited or unlimited time, while polygamy and marriage with close relations is not to be ruled out. It is one of the most significant services to legal philosophy that Hegel brought the true significance of the family as an organic ethical institution to bear in that field.

[72] Already on these grounds the son of the Duke of Sussex, by way of a marriage declared null and void in England, was also denied the right of succession regarding Hannover.

Chapter 1: Marriage

§. 65. The Marriage Bond

<117> The essence of marriage is the *complementarity of the sexes.* The difference between the sexes, and their union as the origin of all new life, is a general law of physical nature. What significance this law has is not a problem of ethics but of natural philosophy.[73] So much is certain, that the sexes are the expression of two general principles of nature, a spiritual generative principle and a material receptive principle. The essence of human marriage, however, is the elevation of these principles and their bond in the *character of the personal.*

Natural *principles* here become personified inasmuch as gender difference is not merely a difference of physical constitution but also of ethical spiritual

---

[73]Compare Schelling, *On the Relation of the Real and the Ideal in Nature,* Hegel, *Encyclopedia,* Pt. I, §§. 220, 221, pt. II, §§. 367, 368. But who is of the opinion that the mystery of the sexes and procreation is revealed through these and similar expositions? I withdraw (and did so already in the second edition) my own deduction of marriage drawn in the first edition [*The Philosophy of Law According to the Historical Perspective: Volume II: Christian Doctrine of Law and State*]. Certainly the sense that was imputed to the incautious expression on p. 244 is not there; the entire conception is not any the less erroneous for that reason, since I placed in God Himself what only belongs to the creation. [Here is the passage in question: Private law comprehends these relationships: mutual recognition of personality, property*, and family. In them together man's godlike nature is fully revealed. For man's personality is the image of the divine, man's property* corresponds to the creation, family to God's eternal begetting. Together they form the kingdom of man. These relationships have their purpose and their fulfillment in themselves, they are not there, as the most recent philosophical school teaches, to serve the state, to be subsumed in it. God wills man and his well-being and perfection for man's sake, not for His own sake. But just as man should and can only be blessed and perfect when enveloped and fulfilled by God, so private law is encompassed and permeated by public law. State and church give him his sanction, they give him his norms, they finally give him guarantee and real protection. And the beginning of all private law, personality and legal capacity, have a place in public law, just as its conclusion and end, legal prosecution, returns to public law].

determinateness, through which in particular the gender characteristic of the woman becomes a specific virtue (modesty, maternal love, etc.) and the union of the sexes at the same time becomes a mutual impulse and support **<118>** of ethical spiritual essence. The *bond itself* however becomes personified in that it is elevated from the mere union of sexual functions into the union of persons for which the former only serves as substrate, thus into a bond not of mere momentary complementarity but of the persons concerned immutably becoming as one in feeling, knowledge, and will, into a *living union*.[74]

Marriage is therefore a bond of love, however *love of a specific sort*, namely complementarity, and so has as its final ground the insufficiency of one's own existence and therefore mutual need, physical and spiritual. Furthermore, it is for this reason not a primarily ethical relation but a *natural relation elevated into the ethical*, which for that reason has natural functions as its necessary basis. It is the transfiguration of nature, the culmination of the physical process of creation, just as the church, as the bond between Christ and the congregation out of which spiritual life springs, is the transfiguration of spiritual relations.

Accordingly, marriage is necessarily *monogamy*. Polygamy does not allow for such mutual devotion, such a thorough union of persons. As such, it is contrary to the essence of marriage and the right of the wife. In it, the husband cannot entirely devote himself to any of the wives, nor can the wife devote herself entirely to the husband, in that she cannot make his love for the other women into her own. Polygamy belongs to that stage of nature in which the full character of personality is lacking, and where on the other hand fertility is the main goal. Man sank back into this stage; "from the beginning it was not so." It therefore has no climatic justification, for the highest ethical relations of man cannot depend on climate; it only has world-historical license during earlier periods, in accordance with the leading of Provi- **<119>** dence. But precisely because of this, once true ethics is revealed it can no longer be regarded as having such. Justifiably did the church, upon converting polygamous peoples, always insist that the husband only maintain the first woman he married and separate from the others.

---

[74]Regarding the climax of nature with respect to the physical process of procreation, see Steffens, *Anthropology*, Vol. 2, pp. 214, 222, 234.

§. 66. The Elements of Marriage

Accordingly, the purpose (τέλος) of marriage is the *complete personal union* of both spouses upon the foundation of sexual union, to which procreation is linked. It therefore has a goal outside of itself, the begetting of children; but its first and sole independent goal lies in itself, the union of the spouses. Therefore the sterile marriage is no less binding and sanctified than the fertile one. The contrary viewpoint, which only recognizes the begetting of children as a positive goal and attributes to marriage itself only a negative goal, to guard against fornication, does not attribute to marriage its full right and ignores its positive goal, the life union of the spouses.[75] This may also be related to the exaggerated preference attached to celibacy, even apart from the spiritual order.

The juristic concept of marriage is the union of both sexes in a *complete life and legal community.* Accordingly, marriage is:

1. *Sexual community* (**conjunctio maris et feminae**). This is an essential aspect of marriage, although by virtue of the ethical nature of man it is only the *basis*, not the actual *content* of the same. For this reason, its later cessation (**imponentia superveniens**) does not impair the marriage, and even in the case of <120> its absence from the start, the consent of the spouses establishes a valid marriage, only without the effect of indissolubility marriage otherwise has; this latter might be termed a *naturally incomplete* marriage. Where however the union of sexes is lacking not only in individual instances but is impossible by general natural laws, there cannot and should not be a marriage.[76]

2. *Life community* (**consortium omnis vitae**), that is, the community of livelihood, household, domicile, sharing in prosperity and adversity. The ethical

---

[75]Extremely precisely expressed, e.g., *Tancred.*, Wund. edition, p. 61: "**Omne matrimonium aut causa suscipiendi prolis aut causa incontinentiae fit**" [Every marriage is either for the purpose of bearing children or for the purpose of incontinence]. This of course is based on isolated biblical texts, but these do not have the intention of comprehensively expressing the essence of marriage.

[76]This is the basis for the prohibition on the marriage of eunuchs. Roman law (Justinian, *Digest*, 23.3.39.1, de jure dot., also compare 1.7.9, J. de adopt.) understands it according to its logical aspect: the concept of marriage is lacking in it; canon law (Bull. magn. II. 634) does so according to its ethical aspect: sexual union without the natural purpose of marriage is sin and offense.

nature of human marriage only exists in this full life community. It therefore may not by way of exception (for a specific marriage) be forsaken, be relinquished by contract as with the physical basis, otherwise the concept of marriage is abolished.

3. *Legal community* (**juris communicatio**), that is, the community of rank, class, legal domicile, bequest to children. This legal community can by way of exception be lacking in important relations. So for example in our unequal marriage (misalliance, morganatic marriage). One may characterize this as a *civil incomplete marriage.*[77]

Marriage thus has a natural, an ethical, and a civil element. **<121>**

§. 67. The Role of Consent

As a bond of personal union, marriage can only be effected by the persons to be joined together, through their act of union, "consent." The motive behind this action (physical attraction, paternal authority, considerations of rank, personal attraction) is the business of subjective morality. Even so, part of the concept and legal order of marriage is that it is validly solemnized only through *free consent*. For all that, however, marriage itself is still *by no means a contract*, in that it stands, not under the spouses, but over them; it has a norm, content, and binding power not through them but through its own ethical nature, and since this is not based on their will, it cannot be abolished by them either. Not only the ethical but also the legal effects of marriage – common domicile, mutual aid, etc. – are far from being the effects of contract. They also undeniably come about according to the nature of marriage. Even the consent (consensus) upon which the *solemnization* of marriage is based is distinguished from other contracts in that it does not comprise individual provision under protection of separate interests but nothing less than a complete devotion of the person (see above, §. 54). By all means is the marriage ceremony subject to the juristic principles regarding consent (e.g., invalidity of coerced consent, etc.); but these

[77] Morganatic marriage etc. is falsely picked out (already from J. H. Böhmer onward) nearly universally as an example of **matrimonium ratum sed non legitimum** [see n. 89]. But it is just as much **legitimum**. Such an example is instead formed by marriage without parental consent in accordance with Roman Catholic canon law. Morganatic marriage is only **civiliter imperfectum**. In the same manner, one may designate *mixed marriage* as an *ecclesiastical incomplete* marriage.

principles nevertheless are essentially modified in consideration of the special nature of *this* consent and the nature of marriage itself (e.g., restricted effect of error, impermissibility of conditions, determination of time, etc.).

§. 68. The Role of Religion

Marriage is primarily and on the whole an *ethical* and *civil* **<122>** relation, not a religious one.[78] For it serves the purpose of maintaining humanity in itself to give it completed shape, not to bind men to God (Book I [*Philosophical Foundations*], §§. 24 and 25). To this end it stands primarily and on the whole under the ordering power of the state and not the church. For all that, it has no less a relation to religion and the church, and that is a dual one, a truly religious or *ritual* and a *dogmatic.*

1. Marriage has *firstly* a *religious*, i.e., *ritual character.*

Already the miracle of procreation embedded in nature produces the consciousness of the proximity and love of God to the creature, which explains the idolatry in pagan cults. In human marriage, the ethical miracle of full personal union of spouses is erected on the foundation of this natural miracle, which in Christian doctrine is even referred to as the symbol of the bond between Christ and the church. This, as true ethical union, as union in pure love, standing over natural inclination and its mutability, can however go on in no other manner than in the innermost focal point of human personality, in the bond with God, i.e., only owing to the spouses joining with each other in God and He with them in immediate proximity. Here, where that which is ethical involves the person himself and his entire devotion as a person, appears its inseparability from that which is religious (Book I [*Philosophical Foundations*], §. 24). This proximity of God and the human need for God's blessing are therefore that which lends marriage its religious character. Pursuant to this, it is also to be solemnized by **<123>** the church and under its blessing and not through the spouses alone or merely

[78] The description of marriage as a "*civil* relationship" has absolutely nothing in common with its description as a "*contractual* relationship." The civil order, and in particular the ethical order upon which it is based, entails requirements regarding the will and the agreement of parties in the same degree as does the religious order. This is quite often confused, however, especially by Catholic writers, who then oppose the *contractual* character instead of the *civil* character to the ecclesiastical character of marriage (the sacrament).

by the civil ruling authority (civil marriage). With a mere civil marriage, then, no religious sentiment is actually assuaged or satisfied, and already from the first ages of Christianity the ecclesiastical union was considered to be a requirement of a true marriage ceremony.

For all that, however, marriage is still not in any way a *sacrament*. For it is not the means of bringing the spouses closer to God, to augment their religiosity, thus not a *means for the benefit of religion*, but vice versa, religion (the bond with God) is here the means to fulfilling and transfiguring the human relation. The divergence of the two churches here is based admittedly in the first place on a discrepancy of the concepts one attaches to the word "sacrament." The Catholics label as sacrament every visible relation to which an invisible divine grace attaches, while the Protestants only label those institutions sacraments which serve as signs and seals of the redemption purposes of the new covenant. To this degree it is only a verbal dispute. But the combination of marriage with baptism and the Lord's Supper indicates that in consequence of that concept marriage is conceived not as a *human relation in need of grace* and assured of grace, but is itself a *means of grace*, is conceived as a relation aimed at religion and redemption.[79] This conception has significant practical consequences. One of these is the strengthening of the indissolubility, without exception, of the bond; for indissolubility by all means exists entirely independently of the concept of the sacrament, is based upon entirely different biblical texts and even is historically more ancient, but **<124>** it is confirmed by it, in that a sacrament as indelible sign (**signum indelebile**) may sometimes be repeated but cannot be abolished. A further consequence is the maintenance of marriages which otherwise would have to be considered null and void (e.g., by error regarding the pregnancy of the bride). Finally however and mainly, the claim to *exclusive jurisdiction of the church* regarding the *validity* of the marriage is based primarily on this conception. For if marriage truly is a means of grace in this sense, like baptism and the Lord's Supper, it is entirely in accordance herewith that only the church and by

---

[79]In this therefore the opposition between Protestant and Catholic doctrine by no means consists in Protestants only recognizing "the *natural* sanctity and divine *consecration* of the married state," as Walter (*Textbook of Canon Law*, §. 288) represents it. The *divine foundation* of marriage is also taught by Protestants.

no means the state can judge and determine regarding the requirements and the existence, that is, the efficacy of it.

2. *Secondly*, marriage also has a *dogmatic character*.

Marriage is the primeval relation of human existence, more ancient than any civil order, even more ancient according to our Christian faith than the limitations of the earthly condition, that is to say, established by God in paradise. But from the beginning it had inviolable divinely sanctioned laws. Now that man finds himself outside of God, consciousness of these commands is yet maintained only in the church, as the conserver of the immediate divine revelation.[80] For this reason, although the church in the Christian state is not the lawgiver regarding marriage such that the legal arrangement must issue from it and be validated in civil life by its authority – this is the affair of the state – even so, what the church attests to be such unchangeable divine law (**jus divinum**) and maintains as such within its ambit, is the insuperable norm and limit for the legislation of the Christian state.

Besides, beyond these laws as divinely attested it certainly befits the church that it, by virtue of its power of educa- **<125>** tion, itself issues directives regarding the validity and permissibility of marriage. But that which the church in this latter capacity, and thus according to its own human insight, arranges (e.g., the **forma Tridentini**) it cannot proclaim as an inviolable rule vis-à-vis the state. Accordingly, the state should not declare valid those marriages which the church by **jus divinum** (dogmatically) declares invalid, but in its legislation it may ignore hindrances that it considers dispensable (e.g., the fourth degree of consanguinity); concessions which the church in its judgment wishes to make and in general may make, the state may unconditionally require of the church (e.g., allowance of the Tridentine form, unconditional provision of assistance or proclamation, etc., regarding mixed marriages). All of this it may do lawfully. Whether it acts wisely in this is another question, which can only be answered in each individual case.

Conversely, the church may not refuse the arrangements regarding the validity of marriage made by the state from ethical and civil considerations where

[80] It is true that the church itself in this regard diverges or vacillates within itself. But the essential ethical form of marriage is everywhere preserved in it, and is nowhere to be found outside of it.

they do not conflict with that divine law. As everyone knows, a great dispute is taking place in the Catholic church regarding this issue. The Curia does not concede any effect regarding ecclesiastical validity to regulations concerning the validity of marriage established by the secular ruling authority (e.g., requirement of parental or governmental/royal consent), since marriage, it being a sacrament, comes only under its jurisdiction. A more moderate party (Gallican) vindicates the right of the state to establish such regulations with ecclesiastical effect on the grounds that the civil contract indirectly is material for the sacrament, because where the civil contract is invalid (which the Curia does not dispute) the sacrament likewise does not extend.[81] In favor of the Curia, **<126>** this has been countered especially by Walter, that "the substance of the sacrament is the *natural* and not the civil contract," thus in judgment of the sacrament the positive arrangements of the state cannot receive any consideration. This argumentation, upon which the entire decision in the final analysis depends, evidently presupposes the principle that everywhere where the natural elements of the marriage contract, consent and in any case consummation, are present, and a divine prohibition does not exist, there the sacrament irrefutably steps in. But this principle refutes the Curia's own proceedings, in that *it itself issues human-positive arrangements* apart from which those natural elements would have no effect, thus especially the entire Tridentine form (**parochus ordinarius, duo testes**). If it is no divine commandment that each naturally concluded marriage of necessity be a sacrament, but rather the church can in human wisdom, for the sake of praiseworthy order, establish conditions of sacraments, such as the

---

[81]Most clearly in Héricourt, *The Ecclesiastical Laws of France,* P. III c. 5 art. 2: "Comme le sacrement de mariage a pour fondement le consentement mutuel des parties — — — ce contrat est en même temps civil et spirituel. D'où il faut conclure, que les souverains peuvent mettre des empêchements au mariage, non pas en donnant atteinte directement au sacrement; mais en déclarant nul le contrat civil, *sans lequel il ne peut y avoir de sacrement"* [As the sacrament of marriage is founded on the mutual consent of the parties, this contract is both civil and spiritual. From this it must be concluded that sovereigns can impede marriage, not by directly undermining the sacrament, but by declaring the civil contract null and void, without which there can be no sacrament]. In the same manner in Theiner: "Variae doctor. cathol. opinion. de jure statuend. etc." in extensive implementation, and in many others.

presence of two witnesses, then there is no ground why it should not concede this to the state as well.[82] Instead, therefore, the material of the sacrament is the natural and *at the same time ethically permissible* marriage contract. Ethically permissible it is <127> not, however, where a well-proportioned civil or ecclesiastical regulation runs counter to it.[83]

Where however, as in the German Lutheran countries, church government is joined with the state power in the princes, thus where a separate church order is lacking, just for that reason the church there is to be accorded a concurrency with the state, at least if the state wishes to answer to its Christian character. Even at the present time, where Protestant marriage laws no longer form part of the church order but are promulgated in the civil code, they nonetheless ought to be enacted with the prior attestation of the church (approval of the synods, consistories, faculties, and the like). Should in the meantime the prevailing condition of public mores and opinion demand some other arrangement, then it ought to be possible for the church to make a statement for itself regarding which marriages it attests to be permissible or otherwise in accordance with the divine Word, and in no way may an unconditional sanction be required from the church, viz. [bez.] its servants, for mere state laws. The prince, in our consti-

---

[82]Already prior to the Council of Trent, the church in this respect could be opposed in its extension of the prohibition of marriage to degrees not divinely prohibited. Should the church through such a positive arrangement hinder the admittance of the sacrament, where after all the natural contract of marriage was present and no divine law opposed, why could not the state do this as well, through positive arrangement, e.g., that parental consent be required?

[83] According to the confession of the early church, marriage concluded by sons [Haussöhne] or slaves without the consent of the father or master was not a marriage but a "**fornicatio**," therefore also no sacrament; should not the same hold true for marriages concluded by subjects against the laws of their ruling authority? However, neither the state nor the church should lightly establish such requirements which do not lie in general natural ethical principles but are of a mere positive-legal character (e.g., approval of a superior for someone in the military, of the sovereign for members of princely households), as disuniting impediments to marriage. They should restrict positive-legal disuniting impediments to marriage primarily to the form of public composition, through which in fact all other considerations most certainly can be preserved.

tution the organ also of the church for its binding statements and regulations, currently issues no statements and regulations anymore as organ of the church; for this he must have consulted the church itself (consistories, synods, etc.); instead, <128> he issues these merely as legislator of the state. Thus, in this matter the church in actuality has had its mouth shut; it has been made impossible for it to issue any regulation, in fact any guidance for its members.

In the same manner as with legislation and on the same grounds, *jurisdiction* over affairs of marriage is primarily and with legal effect a matter for the state. The consequence of the sacrament concept certainly leads to the conclusion that only the church can judge regarding the invalidity of marriage or divorce. But the true nature of marriage as a likewise religious relation does not remove it from civil jurisdiction but only requires that this religious dimension be protected. One such concerns the religious influence on the spouses, in the antecedent spiritual admonition and attempt at reconciliation; another concerns the ecclesiastical soundness of the verdict in the mixed courts: consistories, contemporary Württemberg marriage courts, etc. With respect to this latter, the Christian or [bez.] denominational [konfessionelle] confession of the judge can serve if need be as sufficient guarantee, when for the rest the laws themselves agree with the doctrine of the church. Beyond this, the church's disciplinary maintenance of the religious commandments regarding marriage and pastoral influence and discipline can never be taken away by the jurisdiction of the state. It is only the *legal* consequence which must be enforced by the secular jurisdiction. However, it comports with the sanctity of the marriage bond and the dignity of the publicly recognized church for the state to vest ecclesiastical courts with its authority to this end.

§. 69. The Role of the Civil Order

As long as the church was persecuted by the state, conflict over legislation regarding marriage did not yet arise. <129> Both institutions pursued their separate paths. The secular power, as is self-evident, had no regard for the church, and the church maintained in its sphere its ethical commands regarding marriage without concern for secular legislation, through ecclesiastical means, penance and excommunication. Even after the Byzantine empire assumed the Christian confession, no essential change took place in this, as would have been expected. The clear awareness regarding the connection of state and church was lacking, the malleability for shaping the national condition as yet lacked the

Christian principle. It therefore took quite some time before the Christian principles of marriage passed into *legislation* in any degree at all; the church strove after this, and rightly so, but without success.[84] So for example divorce by mutual agreement and by reason of barrenness of the wife were only abolished by Justinian in a later ordinance, and divorce for imprisonment not at all. The legislative *authority* in marriage matters was however simply and indisputably vested in the emperor. Even the ordinances of Theodosius and Justinian, who bore true Christian sentiment, were issued through pure imperial omnipotence and discretion, apart from any cooperation of the church.

By contrast, in the Western kingdoms the Roman church asserted legislation and jurisdiction over marriage, and that by divine authorization. Not merely the principles, which it attested as divine regulations, but also its own human arbitrary ordinances had unconditional validity, and conversely the secular power issued no command regarding the validity of mar- **<130>** riage. But more than this: the entire legal order and civil validity of the bond of marriage rested exclusively and immediately on its *authority;* the secular ruling authority had no share in this but was simply directed to maintain and execute by means of its external power (**brachium saeculare**) what the church established or judicially decided.

The resistance of the Reformers was directed against this as well as against the content of then-existing ecclesiastical legislation. It is by no means the divine order for the church to have exclusive jurisdiction over affairs of marriage; the secular ruling authority has jurisdiction just as well, and in fact the latter has the duty to issue marriage statutes when the church proceeds against God's Word and Christian freedom, as was actually the case regarding divorce, spiritual kinship,[85] etc. It never came into the Reformers' minds, however, to proclaim marriage to be purely a secular affair, standing only under civil considerations and

---

[84]Here belongs in particular the decision of the African synod (c. 4. C. 32 qu. 7). The "**in qua causa legem imperialem petendam promulgari**" [an imperial law was requested to be promulgated in which case] could not possibly have the meaning, as Eichhorn (*Ecclesiastical Law*, p. 299) states it, of getting the imperial law to recognize ecclesiastical penance, because that would not have occurred to the synod, but rather the meaning of getting the ecclesiastical law of marriage to be sanctioned civilly.

[85][Marriage hindrance centering on the godparent relationship.]

not under religious commands, or that the testimony of the church regarding divine laws of marriage is not a binding norm for the legislation of the state, or that jurisdiction is more appropriately exercised by the secular than the spiritual authority. In fact, the contrary is emphatically the case.[86] To state expressly that there is an immutable commandment of God for marriage would not have occurred to them, since at that time it was self-evident; but in all their discussions and even in their exhortations to the princes to act against Catholic statutes, they actually invoke a divine command. Thus, even when Luther in many of his private expressions declares marriage to be a "secular affair" the connection and the perspective thereof was for the clergy not to "govern" directly therein but for that which in **<131>** reality stands under human discretion (**humani juris**), and at the same time until then was largely conducted by the church, be left to the secular authorities or the mores of the country, such as, e.g., whether at nuptials one should attend services once or twice, how often public notice of the upcoming marriage is to be given.[87] On the other hand, Luther is far from leaving the decision as to whether the innocent party is free to remarry after divorce, or whether one may "repudiate his wife due to leprosy or bad breath," to the discretion of the secular ruling authority separated from the church. Rather, in this regard he himself gave inviolable ecclesiastical testimonial.[88] Regarding marriage courts, however, the Reformers spoke the same principle under all conditions, that they should be ecclesiastical and not secular courts, and held the consistories to be the most expedient. Thus the sense of the Reformers is neither

---

[86] Compare my *The Church Constitution According to the Doctrine and Law of Protestants*, 1st ed., p. 74.

[87] Luther's *Complete Writings,* X. 854. "The saying goes, 'as many countries, as many customs.' Thus, since the marriage ceremony and the married state are a *secular affair*, our ministers and sextons have nothing in that regard to order or *govern*, but to leave to each city and country its usage and custom as they are. Some bring the bride twice to the church, both in the evening and in the morning, some only once, some announce and invite from the pulpit two or three weeks prior. I allow the lords and councils to create and make such-like as they wish, it is none of my concern. But if it is desired of us that we bless them before the church or in the church, or pray over them, or marry them, we are obligated to do that."

[88] Luther's *Complete Writings,* X. 797.

to separate the content of marriage law from the doctrines of faith and testimonies of the church, nor to exclude ecclesiastical cooperation in its arrangement and upholding, but only the restoration of the state in that supreme and sole legal authority which befits it in that matter, and the freedom to make human praiseworthy ordinances beyond the divine commandments, which up until then the church had presumed to do. **<132>**

This intention is also confirmed by subsequent actual arrangement in Protestant countries, which undeniably springs from it. This is based on the connection of secular and ecclesiastical power in the person of the sovereign, which eliminated the conflict[89]; but even so, marriage was predominantly treated as an affair of the church, the confession of faith was considered its supreme guide, its arrangement was issued by the church government, effected in the church ordinances, not in the national statutes, thereby on the advice of the ecclesiastical organs since the consistories had jurisdiction.

Only since the time of Thomasius did the viewpoint gain ground, partly from misunderstanding the Reformers, that marriage is a secular matter and as such solely the responsibility of the civil ruling authority. A similar development has proceeded in the Catholic countries since the Josephine era.[90] Finally, the

---

[89]Accordingly, a division into **matrimonium ratum** [answering to ecclesiastical requirements] and **legitimum** [answering to secular legal provisions] formally is not possible. Nevertheless, materially it remains of importance. For example, there are now countless marriages which are **matrimonia legitima** and yet not **matrimonia rata** according to the principles of the Protestant church. Marriages which are not **matrimonia legitima** and yet **rata** do not exist because the Protestant church does not grant ecclesiastical sanction to a civilly inadmissible marriage. But the concept of a **matrimonium non legitimum** and yet **ratum** could become applicable in the case of the state not merely setting requirements for the validity of marriage but also mandating absolute prohibitions on marriage, in particular to the extent that they abolish those of Christian freedom as advocated by Protestants, for example, when marriage is declared by state law to be indissoluble in terms of the marriage bond even for Protestants, as was done in France, or marriage is denied to priests who have gone over to the Protestant church, etc. J. H. Böhmer and others therefore have no grounds for describing this distinction as something purely Catholic, which Protestants must abandon.

[90][A reference to the reign of Emperor Joseph of Austria (1780-1790).]

newer philosophic doctrine conceives of marriage as a purely civil relation, in fact as a mere contractual relation. Thus in recent times in many states the conversion has come not only in *formal* perspective, that the determinations regard- <133> ing the marriage bond form part of the civil code and fall under the jurisdiction of the civil courts – against which, under the modifications indicated in §. 68, nothing can be objected – but in *material* perspective as well, that legislation has been entirely detached from the Christian teaching regarding marriage.[91]

The three most recent major codes of law, the Austrian, Prussian and French, have the *formal* principle in common that legislation and jurisdiction in matrimonial matters emanate solely from the state. In their *material* principle, however, they are essentially different. The Austrian has the principle of the indissoluble *union* of church and state, i.e. of ecclesiastical and civil marriage, the other two equally, but to different degrees, that of *separation*, which is why the former is calculated for Catholics and contains a special arrangement for Protestants, whereas the latter are merely given as such for all subjects without any consideration of confession. The *Austrian civil code* vests all marriage legislation and jurisdiction exclusively in the sovereign and, in particular, in the secular courts. Indeed, it goes so far as to declare its civil legislation binding *in foro interno*, i.e. with regard to the sacrament, and therefore to compel the clergy to consecrate, dispense and so on. But for this it also follows Catholic dogma in its content, in such a way that it strictly complies with the provisions which the Roman Church declares to be a *jus divinum*, e.g. the non-dispensable degrees of kinship, indissolubility. On the other hand, it does not recognize the merely human orders of the Church as binding, abolishes, for example, the dispensable diriment impediments as well as in many cases the merely impedient impediments and itself sets requirements for the validity of the marriage (diriment impediments), e.g. consent of parents, guardians, military leaders. It thus subjects ecclesiastical ministers and authorities to secular jurisdiction, but never forces them to act contrary to the faith of the Church, because that which is the faith of the Church is its guide.

---

91 [The following three paragraphs were not included in the first edition of this translation.]

The *Prussian civil code*, on the other hand, takes no account at all of the church in its content, and therefore contains a number of provisions that contradict the faith of Protestants no less than that of Catholics, e.g. divorce on the grounds of dislike or mutual consent, on the grounds of disgusting illness, etc. In contradiction to this, however, it makes the involvement of the church, the marriage ceremony, a condition of marriage. This leads to the alternative: either the clergy is forced to marry contrary to what it recognizes as a *divine* prohibition, which is violation of conscience, or the clergy is allowed to follow its conscience, in which case the code is illusory. In relation to Catholics, the latter has already been implemented by law. Obviously, however, this is not consistent with the fact that the state, through its code of law, allows Catholic subjects a number of marriages that are not permitted by the church, from the state's point of view guarantees them to a certain extent; on the other hand, by requiring the marriage ceremony while releasing the priest from the law, it renders them virtually impossible again. But the reprehensible thing lies in the former provision. If the Protestant clergy, as it can demand, were now also to be granted the same, which can hardly be withheld any longer, the entire legislation would be without effect.

The *French Code* consistently implements the separation of the secular and the spiritual which the Prussian Territorial Law contains only incompletely, and therefore does not, like the latter, arrive at that alternative. In the content of its provisions, it likewise takes no account of religious statutes (although it does not permit such arbitrary divorces as Prussian law); however, neither does it require marriage ceremonies, but allows marriage to be solemnized by the civil authorities – *civil marriage*.

This separation of the secular and the spiritual everywhere had the same defect: it placed a dichotomy between state and church, which were harmoniously to foster the human race, in that the state would sanction marriages which the members of one of the officially recognized churches solemnized under the faith and commandments of that church. It is the declaration of the profanation of marriage and therefore weakens, to the degree that it has an effect, the consciousness of marriage's sanctity and God-given ordinances. It leads to marriage legislation of lesser strictness and purity. The French civil code is still strict to a degree, in consequence of Catholic custom and the reaction against the previous period of general dissolution; but it is by no means derived from pure principles appropriate to the ethical essence of marriage; above all, the marriage statutes of the Prussian civil code run to the extreme opposite of strictness and purity. The expected advantage, that civil marriage would eliminate the conflict between church and state and thus a great deal of confusion, is only apparent. For the conflict then shifts to another area, between the church and its members, which excommunicates them in the absence of state intervention, and between the two confessions. This conflict would be much more appropriately and fundamentally eliminated if the civil legislation were brought into closer correspondence with the ecclesiastical, than when it is separated from it. The actual motivation behind civil marriage does not however lie in such <134> advantages, but simply in Christianity being recognized not as the public faith of the nation and the authoritative power in the state, but merely as a private conviction of individuals, and indeed here alone lies the decision for ecclesiastical or civil marriage. The civil solemnization of marriage (not civil marriage in general) is appropriate as an exception, to wit, in relation to sects which the state tolerates, but the clergy of which cannot be extended public authority to solemnize valid marriages.[92]

---

[92]Civil marriage as introduced in England by the legislation of William IV and Queen Victoria is something entirely different from civil marriage in the sense of the Continent. The occasion and goal there was only the liberation of dissenters from being forced to have their marriages solemnized by the state church. The civil character therefore extends only to the solemnization of marriage and not to the marriage laws and jurisdiction; these have retained their ancient Christian character, and even the civil solemnization of marriage does not consist in the marriage being solemnized through a civil act of a civil servant – this only takes place through the highest registering official (superintendent registrar) in London, who certainly is only seldom approached – but through dissenting clerics through religious rites answering to their congregation, albeit concluded in the presence of secular officials (registrars) along with two witnesses, and certified by them. Beyond this, the clerics of the state church and the religious communities which previously were hereto entitled (Jews and Quakers) do not even require civil participation, but as yet solemnize marriage merely through the religious act, in legally valid fashion. With regard to lists of marriages, as with those of baptisms (births) and deaths, the clergy of the state church, where they still draw up these lists, is required

§. 70. Restriction on Marriage: Near Relationship

The true restriction of marriage is *near relationship,* which general human sentiment testifies has a necessary ground in the ethical order. The point is to declare the following: **<135>**

Near relationship, in particular parental, and marriage are relationships separated by God in nature. As the physical bond is specific to each, so is the bond of love. They therefore cannot be mixed with each other. The primary ethical bonds can be amassed in infinity, e.g., love of neighbor, friendship, gratitude, teacher and student; but the natural organic relations with their specific significance are exclusive. The Old Testament puts it like this: "Thou shalt not sow your fields with two seeds, shalt not weave wool and linen together," etc., which expresses this thought symbolically: Thou shalt not move the boundaries set by God in nature. This is the meaning of our deep ethical revulsion (**horror naturae**) for incest.

Marriage, firstly considered for its own sake, is a bond of necessitous, fulfillment-seeking, yearning love (§. 59). Even aside from all physical aspects, which do in fact belong to its essence, it is, in its purest spiritual relationships, based on a need for completion, is only satisfied through reciprocation, and seeks the continuous effectuation thereof. By contrast, the parent-child relationship above all is a bond of elevated, solicitous love which is absolutely in no need (Godlike), on the one hand, and is of the most reverential awe on the other. This bond is completely destroyed and desecrated through the bond of equal need of fulfillment. Marriage between parents and children is therefore an absolute abomination.[93] But the bond between siblings is an *organic* bond of love *without need;* it has the organic purpose of *being* the family, of realizing its goal, not of *generating* the family, of being a means for it. The realized goal of the family is however a

---

to send them to the same supreme civil servant in London, and thus in this respect has been made into a subordinate civil servant. However, such lists are not, as is marriage, an ecclesiastical but a civil affair. Accordingly, marriage in England has retained its ecclesiastical character as it was, even in the most recent legislation; this legislation, in contrast with that on the Continent has a declaration of secularity and the greater relaxation of marriage laws neither as motive nor as consequence.

[93]Even the opinion that without her incest the human race would die out does not for that reason excuse Lot's daughter.

closed circle of those who are bound to each other in communal love for the parents, through equal, non-self-interested, **<136>** non-yearning love amongst each other.[94]

Another motive arises from the significance of marriage to the entirety of the human race, specifically the nation [bez. des Volks]. Within this relationship, marriage has the purpose of supplementing familial individualities [Famileindividualitäten], in so doing generating individualities and effecting a crossing of the human race. Therefore sexual love is already naturally contingent upon the attraction of a different familial individuality (Hegel), and marriage should go outside the family so as to expand the bond of love (Augustine). Accordingly, marriage within the family is an egotistical (narcissistic) involution of the same upon itself, similar to the connection of the same sex. Thus, since more families exist, the bonds separate themselves sharply: marriage as the means to establish the family, which must go outside of itself; the sibling bond as established family, the goal of which is to remain unmixed [unvermischt].

Accordingly, the actual original relationships of incest are those between parents and children and between siblings, each in turn in various manners and degrees.[95] From this point, however, extension takes place according to analogy, once to the relation of "**respectus parentelae**" (uncle and aunt), then to in-laws, since the closest **<137>** bonds, to wit, the bonds of piety, become common to the married couple. For in-laws in direct line, the prohibition on marriage is *unconditionally* based in the nature of the bond. But it is also *appropriate* for the collateral line of the first degree as well (marriage with a brother's widow, the

---

[94]The exception that we must suppose for the children of the first human pair is justified in that they represented not merely the family but at the same time the race. In that case, both aspects are pushed together in the bud, only later to come to separate development. Contrary to this, in terms of the natural order the relation between parents and children can never represent the race.

[95]Even one who rejects the revealed doctrine of the single progenitor of the human race at least cannot take away that, in the case of civilized people, sibling marriage by way of exception, at least between half-brothers and sisters, is recognized (e.g., Abraham, Cimon), but never marriage with parents. Once the race has been extended, both are certainly in the same way and absolutely reprehensible, albeit not in the same way in terms of the idea, thus from the beginning.

sister of the deceased wife), simply to foster the innocence and simplicity of the sibling bond among relatives by marriage. By contrast, that principle of full communication of bonds of mutual relationship derived from the becoming-one-flesh of the two spouses, and according to which the prohibition consequently extends itself everywhere as far as the relationship, even to the in-laws of the other spouses and again the in-law of a spouse previously deceased (relation of marriage of the "second" and "third kind") is to be rejected. Factually, the church has also abandoned this principle. Yet another extension exists for children of siblings in terms of the viewpoint of expanding the bond of love, thus not allowing the family to shut itself up in itself[96]; but further extension beyond children of siblings is exaggeration.

With these extensions, the institution of *dispensation* is appropriate, within limits and properly administered. The objection made to this, that a marriage is either immoral and therefore not amenable to dispensation, or it is not immoral and hence in no need of dispensation, is only apparent. In fact, in accordance with the former consideration it is often only *in general undesirable* for marriages to be contracted among such relatives, that they become customary, **<138>** without that particular marriage being *immoral in itself*, in fact in special cases it could even be desirable and good. Dispensation comes to the aid of such cases. Chiefly, however, the requirement of dispensation maintains the awareness that as general custom such marriages are not the proper social condition. Even so, dispensation is not to take place in relations of marriage of direct descent, nor perhaps, or at least only in the rarest cases, for marriage with one's aunt. Whether it is not more appropriate that many of these marriages subject to dispensation, e.g., among children of siblings, be made lawful, leaving it to

[96]The prohibition of marriage among children of siblings is falsely attributed to the *principle of enclosure* borrowed from rabbinical sources (**"vicinitas gradus prohibiti," "vallum et sepimentum legis divinae"** – Augustine, Melanchthon, Gerhard). It is based on the deeper and truer ground expressed by Augustine, for which reason these marriages were also objectionable to the Romans. Only the wider extension belongs to this, in no way grounded, principle of enclosure.

mores to keep them from becoming too frequent, cannot be subject to any unconditional rule, it depending on the sense of the times.[97] **<139>**

In our view, therefore, the prohibition of marriage has its basis in *the specific nature of the particular organic family ties*, parental and fraternal, and therefore extends only to them and to some equally specific ones which are analogous to them. The church in the Middle Ages, however, followed an essentially different

---

[97] With regard to the prohibition on marriage in general, the *Mosaic law* is by no means to be considered a *particular Jewish* law of God ("**lex positiva**"), as is usually the case in the Protestant church since Michaelis. For it is not concerned with ceremonies, but with an ethical relation; in particular, that the Jews should fall under stricter rules in this regard than Christians runs contrary to the entire relation of the Old and New Covenants, such as is shown e.g. in the command regarding divorce and polygamy. The early church therefore rightly recognized that these rules should rather be more strict than more lax, thus e.g. the prohibition of marriage among children of siblings, as already observed by the Romans. By contrast, the viewpoint held by the earlier Protestant church, and which was also maintained by Catholic theological faculties in Europe in the case of Henry VIII in opposition to the Pope, that the Mosaic law is an *indispensable* divine command, is erroneous. This is already shown in the dispensation of the Levirate marriage expressed in the law itself. In that the Old Testament does not know of dispensation, those relations which are absolutely illicit are left undistinguished from those which are not to constitute regular mores. The standpoint of the Catholic church in this is more true and free than the former rationalistic and the latter orthodox standpoints. For the rest, it is merely the prohibition on marriage with one's aunt and with the (not childless) widow of one's brother, which is the reason why one wishes to consider the Mosaic law as a mere Jewish law. But in those conditions of pure mores, these marriages did not exist as regular usage, in fact the former perhaps was entirely ruled out. It is no coincidence that the Mosaic law prohibits not in terms of descent and degree but according to particular ties. Marriage with one's aunt is less permissible than with one's uncle, because the relation of reverence is reversed; marriage with one's brother's widow is less permissible than with one's wife's sister, since in the latter case the woman already belonged to the man's family. This is because in marriage the wife enters into the family of the husband and not vice versa – a distinction which in ancient conditions (not only Jewish) certainly had greater significance, but which never entirely disappears. That Levirate marriage is a merely Jewish institution is self-evident.

view, misled by a misunderstanding of the Mosaic Law. It found the reason for the prohibition of marriage, without regard to the organization of the family and its particular vocational positions, to be *kinship* (consanguinity) *in general.* Accordingly, the prohibition of marriage has no limit other than that which is arbitrarily set for trivial reasons, such as the analogy of the seven ages of the world or the four humors in the human body. The boundless excess to which one has progressed is therefore not based on a merely quantitatively incorrect determination, but on an incorrect principle.[98]

In earlier times, one used to list a variety of grounds for the prohibition of incest, as for example Thomas Aquinas.[99] In more recent times, by contrast, the viewpoint (already listed by Aquinas) came to dominate, through the efforts of Michaelis, whereby the prohibition merely has the goal of hindering seduction which otherwise threatens among persons in such close contact. This goal, although certainly attained, cannot be the ground of the prohibition; a mere rule of prudence cannot bring about such a deep shudder. The concurrence of the prohibition of marriage with the allowance for unveiled encounters is certainly a poor argument that the former of necessity derived from the latter rather than the reverse. Even the Augustinian explanation from the viewpoint of expanding the bond of love[100] is insufficient in itself in that it, at least in its expression, is

---

[98] [This paragraph was not included in the first edition of this translation.]

[99] Aquinas, *Summa theolog.* 2.2. qu. 154, art. 9. A good critical exposition in particular with regard to more recent viewpoints is contained in the *Evangelical Church Gazette* [Evangelische Kirchenzeitung], June 1840.

[100] "Habita est ratio rectissima caritatis, ut hominibus, quibus esset utilis atque honesta concordia, diversarum necessitudinum vinculis necterentur, nec unus in una multas haberet, sed singulae spargerentar in singulos" [The demands of charity are most perfectly satisfied by men uniting together in the bonds that the various ties of friendship require, so that they may live together in a useful and becoming amity; nor should one man have many relationships in one, but each should have one – in *De Civitate Dei,* ch. XV, 16]; furthermore the **multiplicatio amicorum** being disregarded. The *Evangelical Church Gazette* cited above maintains this to be the true explanation, for the reason that it justifies so conclusively the exception of the *first* siblings. Even so, in return it includes the shortcoming that according to it Lot's daughters – under the condition of the error that they alone were left – acted entirely properly.

only based on considerations of expediency. In that it completely abstracts from the specificity of the family tie, it leads logically to unlimited extension, as forthwith took place.

In that regard, Hegel[101] rightly postulated an absolute <140> ground, although he unjustifiably looks for this merely in the fact that marriage as the free devotion of both sexes should not be concluded in already familiar (naturally identical) circles, but calls for various mutually unfamiliar individualities which then first join with each other into a community. According to this explanation, marriage between mother and son is only reprehensible because each lacks the charm of novelty. The horror of incest is however not so much or not merely a feeling that it does not do marriage justice but rather that it violates bonds of relation and piety. Much more appropriate is therefore the ground proposed by Aquinas as primary, and lately by Nitzsch, as the actual ground, that man owes his parents (and in consequence those initially descending from those parents) reverence, that this reverence is contrary to fleshly commingling, which always entails a certain shame ("turpitudo"). But this ground is not completely understood should one merely recognize in it the physical expression of marriage, which one then characterizes as shame, and not rather the innermost essence of marriage, the incompatibility with the parental bond, etc. <141>

---

[101]*Philosophy of Law*, §. 168: "In that, furthermore, this in itself limitless peculiar personality is of both sexes from whose *free devotion* marriage is derived, it therefore must not be concluded within already naturally identical, self-known and familiar circles, in which individuals do not have a personality peculiar to themselves over against each other, but from separated families and originally distinct personality. Marriage among blood relatives is therefore contrary to the concept by which marriage is an *ethical act of freedom*, not a connection of immediate naturalness and its urge." Then: "confidentiality, acquaintance, the custom of shared action is not to come before marriage but is only to be found in it, which has that much higher value the richer it is and the more depth it has." There is furthermore something disconcerting in the fact that Hegel contrasts marriage as an ethical relation, merely because of its *voluntary* union, with kinship as a mere *natural urge*. One might just as well reverse this, and contrast kinship as mere ethical relation to marriage as a natural (because of its ongoing physical basis) relation.

§. 71. The Place of Property in Marriage

In accordance with freedom of disposition, which is the general principle of property*, goods relations among married couples are subject to contractual establishment across a broad sphere. These however find their limit in the fundamental purpose of the family. The law therefore only has to express which forms it recognizes and which, in cases of doubt, are natural.

Marriage has the purpose of uniting the spouses in complete life community, but it does not at all thereby eliminate independent personality. Accordingly, joint property* is to serve the marriage (i.e., to feed the family, raise the children, etc.) in common, and thus to come under the administration of the husband, providing security to the wife where necessary, but in no way coalescing into an undifferentiated mass. A community of use and appropriation, not of rights, is to come about. This is to extend beyond death, so that the surviving members, in particular the wife, is granted an inheritance or in any case a usufruct in greater or lesser extension depending on concurrent interests. German laws are determined by these proper principles.

Accordingly, the *marital community of goods* is by no means founded in the essence of marriage, even though it would seem so at first sight. Its justification instead lies in the requirements of certain estates, in particular the industrial and trading classes, in which property* is also the foundation of the trade, the contracting of debt is part of the regular livelihood, and both spouses customarily take part in the expansion of property* (acquisition) through capital or labor. It is therefore an institution answering only to these classes and not at all in general. By contrast, the *Roman dotal system* is **<142>** not natural in this matter in that it only applies a portion of the property* of the wife to the marriage (**ad matrimonii onera ferenda**), while the remainder of her property is assigned, as it were, to separate enjoyment outside the marriage.

§. 72. Divorce[102]

In accordance with its purpose as the complete personal union of the spouses, marriage is *indissoluble*. A sexual connection with prior intent of dissolution or

[102]Compare *Regarding the Current Shape of Marriage Law* (2nd edition, Berlin, 1842) [author: Otto von Gerlach], my speech concerning the Dobenek motion to restrict

with a condition thereto thus no longer falls under the concept of marriage. But neither may subsequent change of will and sentiment grant entitlement to dissolution, if marriage is to retain its ethical form. *Adultery* forms an exception. For it is not merely the absolute violation of the ethical bond of marriage but it also abolishes marriage's physical basis, sexual union (i.e., exclusive bondedness) among the spouses, and hence is factually and fully the destruction of the marriage. It is then the specific and therefore sole ground of divorce, declared as such in Christ's statement (Matthew 5, etc.). Accordingly, the objection made in recent times from a philosophical standpoint in the Protestant church (Klee), that adultery cannot be generically distinguished from other violations of marriage, is unfounded. The seal of nature is dissolved by adultery, under which the spouses to that point were agreed as "one flesh," which is true of no other violation. The Protestant church is also not the only one to treat that biblical statement regarding adultery as a unicum; the Catholic church like- **<143>** wise restricts the lifetime separation, which divorce represents for it, to the case of adultery, and only allows temporary separation for other violations, such as malicious desertion, attempt on the life of a spouse.[103]

If it is the true form of marriage and thus the goal of civilized, especially Christian peoples, that likewise in the legal order divorce occur only because of

---

divorce in the Bavarian parliamentary hearings [Ständeverhandlungen] of 1837 (supplementary volume, XII, p. 181); Puchta regarding the Prussian draft of a divorce law in *Leaflets for Questions of the Day* (I), Berlin 1843; Savigny, *Representation of the Reform Undertaken in the Prussian Divorce Laws*, Berlin 1844.

[103]That adultery by the wife entitled the husband to divorce but not vice versa is a viewpoint that asserted itself already in the early church. Nor did Justinian (nov. 117) recognize adultery by the husband as in and of itself sufficient grounds for divorce (**repudium**) for the wife, but only when joined with scandal (the husband maintains the concubine in the house or is encountered with her in public multiple times in the same city); the French civil code followed this. Even though adultery by the wife in itself degrades her much more than that by the husband does him, and beyond this renders uncertain relations of descent, still according to Christian acknowledgement adultery by the husband is likewise an absolute violation of the marriage bond, and the sexes stand equally entitled vis-à-vis each other, so that it is not justifiable to legally bind the wife to the marriage after the husband has broken it.

adultery, then the existing condition of mores, which cannot endure such strictness, nevertheless justifies *analogous extensions* of this ground of divorce, to wit, to other *far-reaching fault on the part of the other*, especially where this concerns the marriage bond itself. This is the situation in later Protestant consistorial practice. The older practice allowed no other ground for divorce than adultery and malicious desertion – which it also considered to be a biblical ground – in particular it did not allow serious abuse, lunacy, crime, etc.[104] Since the age of Thomasius and Stryck, however, this was expanded, and beyond these J. H. Böhmer attested as sufficient grounds the refusal of marital duty, intentional sterilization, attempt on the life of a spouse, and lifetime imprisonment or exile. The same standpoint dominates Justinian's legislation (Novel 117). It appears to us to correspond to the contemporary condition for civil legislation. **<144>**

A determinate boundary in terms of this viewpoint cannot be discerned. *Serious fault* however always remains the *insuperable precondition.*[105] Whether the church can agree to analogous extension of the biblical grounds for divorce and such forms of remarriage in the case of divorce is a question belonging to positive theology. The conception of marriage and adultery given here speaks against it, as does the authority of the church itself precisely in the times of deepest Christian earnestness. All the same, to grant such an expansion, not of course as a sanction but nevertheless as an allowance, does not require the church to evoke the separation of civil and ecclesiastical marriage, and it might perhaps thereby preserve the sanctity of the commandment through a form of marriage ceremony which announces the ideas that such a marriage is based not on complete endorsement but only on allowance, as was expressed in the older Protestant church upon every remarriage of the innocent party, even where it occurred due to adultery. And in such cases there was never any coercion put on the clergyman who refused to recognize a divorce on any other grounds than the biblical one. The church government has no authority to do that.

---

[104] Carpzov, *jurispr. consist.* def. 202. Lauterb. *colleg.* I. 24. tit. 2. §. 21.

[105] The decision of the Council of State as reported (p. 57) in the *Representation* cited earlier [n. 102], that "the judge is to determine whether the marriage relation has been broken in no lesser degree by the *offense* than through adultery or malicious abandonment," aptly expresses the principle.

By contrast, altogether contrary to the ethical essence of marriage is divorce due to *unilateral or mutual dissatisfaction, "insuperable enmity," "estrangement of minds,"* when such is not motivated by serious fault on the part of the other party but derived from other grounds (decline in attraction, change in natural affinity, discovered imperfections or even trivial faults in the other spouse, conflicting habits, needs, hobbies, etc.) **<145>** and above all, divorce from mere *mutual agreement*. No less in conflict with the ethical essence of marriage is divorce due to *accident without fault* by the other spouse, such as due to revolting disease, later impotence, etc. These are the two classes of grounds of divorce to be rejected out of hand.[106] With the first, one places the caprice of the spouses or their arbitrary feeling above the ethical bond of marriage, while with the second one sanctions the violation of its supreme requirement, to bear mishaps in common.[107] A marriage that one wishes to uphold only as long as the feeling of affection continues, and one in which in misfortune one abandons one's spouse, is certainly not a true marriage. This is what newer legislation more or less has come to, motivated in part by the inappropriate exclusive foundation of the principle of individual freedom, which came about partly through misapprehended humanity, partly through the looser ethical outlook of the times and the preeminence of outward considerations such as expanding the population. The French civil code only contains one of these categories, that of mutual consent

---

[106] The classification of grounds of marriage: fault [Schuld] – mutual dissatisfaction – unhappiness of one party, and the implementation that only the former but not the two latter are admissible according to ethical principles, form the main content of my speech of 1837 cited above. The same form the principles of the *Representation* of 1844 [n. 102]. For an impartial judgment, this may perhaps be trivial but by no means doubtful. Thus even Wiese (*Textbook of Ecclesiastical Law*, III. 315), who in other things is among the laxest, accepts that only "deliberate violation of the duty of marriage" justifies divorce. Even so, neither my speech in Bavaria in 1837 nor the *Representation* in Prussia of 1844 was able to bring about a change in legislation.

[107] Not only did Luther (Walch X. 724, 797) agitate against such divorce; Kant did so as well (*Doctrine of Law*, p. 110), expressing himself thusly: "Should incapacity only occur afterward, that right can lose nothing through this *innocent coincidence*." Even in the deliberations of the French Council of State under Napoleon, these three classes of grounds for divorce introduced by the law of 1792 found no single defender.

(consentement mutuel), and although this does not <146> correspond to the essence of marriage in principle, nevertheless in terms of result it is without disadvantage due to the gigantic hindrances this places in the way of such divorce. Add to this that the French civil code does not contain most of the grounds of divorce of Protestant consistorial practice, so that mutual consent often only serves in place of material grounds which are obnoxious to judicial treatment. Finally, the French civil code enjoins both parties from remarrying for three years, so that divorce cannot be used as a mere means of satisfying an other-directed inclination. The Prussian civil code, by contrast, introduced both categories, in great extension and without provisos.

Accordingly, if divorce is not otherwise justified than by serious fault, so then is punishment also necessarily visited on the guilty party by the ethical community, state or church, enough so that the blameworthiness is actually attested, that remarriage at least for a specific period be prohibited to him as the one showing himself unworthy of marriage. Divorce can never be considered as a mere episode, as an event for which no one is responsible. If guilt adheres to both parties, then divorce is ruled out altogether; for it is merely a favor to and an entitlement of the innocent party. Thus the church, in consideration of the grounds of marriage which it alone permits, maintains that adultery conducted by both sides cancels each other out, and divorce is not granted. The same must then also hold true when legislation establishes the extension of this ground of divorce to other serious fault, where guilt much more often emerges on both sides.

§. 73. Principle of Marriage: Personal Satisfaction or Higher Order?

Such seriousness regarding grounds for divorce is advis- <147> able even merely from consideration of results. For even lax legislation, if it otherwise does not wish to sink to the level of complete abandonment of the marriage bond, is incapable of coming to the aid of every unhappy marriage. Now on the other hand, it is by means of these fixed principles that the sanctity of the marriage bond in public sentiment is preserved which otherwise is destroyed by the spectacle of facile divorce, and even in individual marriages contentment is often strengthened vis-à-vis temptations brought on by the prospect of arbitrary separation and remarriage. Regarding the latter consideration, the question is whether the number of marriages is greater which, in themselves unhappy, avail themselves of lax marriage laws, or whether the number of these marriages, in themselves happy or at least curable, become unhappy only because of lax marriage laws? The question is whether in fact "insuperable enmity" is not in the majority of cases much rather an unresisted other-directed affection? More decisive however than the consequence is the principle itself. An ethical polity cannot allow the sanctioning of divorce or remarriage which is in conflict with the essence of marriage in order thereby at the cost of mores to provide its members relief for or improvement of its natural well-being. Instead, it has the obligation to register its own, i.e., the national, the state, the ecclesiastical, ethical valuation of marriage in its laws and in the order of the public condition (Book II [*Principles of Law*], §. 6).

Above all, this is confirmed or rather only brought to clear consciousness through the Christian principle. *Christ's statement* regarding divorce is of course *not* a direct *law for the external legal condition* of the state or even of the church, but only for conscience. This is already clear from the preceding parallel statements, which obviously only concern moral relations. Even so, it is a *disclosure of the ethical idea* of the institution of marriage, and this is the principle of legal formation in **<148>** all life relations including this one.[108] From this follows that civil legislation is not to espouse this statement verbatim and in its fullest extent, i.e., merely to implement it, but nevertheless that it must stand on the same basis as it, that it not follow a principle which deviates from it. There is therefore a stricter and a milder implementation of the Christian principle of divorce for civil legislation, both appropriate according to prevailing conditions, the more so because in this matter, legislation does not have the vocation of making known a confession but much rather of exercising an educational power, for which it must of necessity adhere to the given prerequisites. But the Christian state should never put the public legal ordering of divorce under another principle and restrict it to the mere morality of the individual.

In consequence, the *ethical* and the *Christian* principles for divorce (or, as many express it, the "human ethical" and the "divine holy" marriage), which in recent times are set in opposition to each other, not only are not oppositions but in terms of results not even distinctions. There is no ethical principle for marriage apart from the Christian and no positive Christian apart from the ethical. Christianity herein represents mores [Sitte] over against bad customs [Unsitte]

---

[108]Compare Book II [*Principles of Law*], §. 6, and §. 61 above.

precisely world-historically [weltgeschichtlich]. In the entire pagan world, and even in Judaism, marriage in fact was viewed predominantly as a mere *tie of inclination*, especially on the part of the man, and therefore divorce was arbitrary[109]; by contrast, the <**149**> Christian church considered it predominantly as an *ethical bond*, the obligating power of which does not depend on inclination and life satisfaction and can only be dissolved by the most serious blame of the other part. This notion is yet common to both the strictest Roman Catholic discipline and the laxest more recent Protestant praxis, but it is this which is the ethical notion of marriage. It is therefore obviously a regression to pre-Christian bad customs when now once again a widespread viewpoint regarding the *spouses' happiness in life* is made into the absolute principle for divorce. According to it, divorce shall take place where one spouse or both find themselves to be entirely mistaken in their hopes of satisfaction in life even without any serious, yea perhaps without any, blame at all from the one side or the other. The same spouses, reasonable, well-meaning, good-natured, yet leading with each other an intolerable marriage, in that they do not match with each other – these same spouses will be able to swap and establish two happy marriages, why then chain them to each other? Perhaps only a few consciously go so far, but unconsciously it is this manner of viewing things which underlies opposition to that severity of the divorce laws, and the entire opposition of opinions is, reduced to its innermost core, none other than the question whether the *life satisfaction* of the spouses forms the sole and single principle or whether above anything else it will be the *ethical form of marriage* that forms this principle. No compromise is possible

---

[109]Polygamous peoples actually do not come into consideration here at all, in that the husband, for which it is intended, does not have a need for divorce, despite which among these peoples the husband often is entitled to a license of repudiation. With respect to monogamous peoples, the Attic law permitted the arbitrary repudiation of the wife, arbitrary abandonment of the husband, just as the Roman law in unrestricted fashion permitted not only divorce by mutual agreement but, already early on, the unilateral abolition of marriage (**repudium**). The latter did have disadvantages when it occurred without any legally recognized ground; but the sundering of the marriage always followed. Where in that age a restriction on divorce is found, it is based not on the ethical essence of marriage but only on the treatment of the wife as mere thing or on an agnatic or political interest, or a mere ceremony of religion.

with the former viewpoint; such would rest on a stricter or milder interpretation, but yielding here would be tantamount to abandoning the Christian viewpoint altogether on this <150> point. One in that case would have to admit that he postulates not the good but the pleasurable as the principle of social order.

The rationale, finally, that in the case of estrangement of minds the marriage bond as bond of love is already abolished and therefore that divorce is only the legal expression of an existing fact, is based on the confusion of *natural* and *ethical love.* The former is located in sentiment and therefore is mutable, arbitrary, while the latter is located in the will and ought not change; the former is a form of luck [ein Schicksal] that strikes people, the latter is an act which depends on their freedom. It is however precisely the essence of marriage to elevate the bond of mere sentiment into the ethical bond of the will. Marriage certainly has sentiment as its basis, for which reason sentiment is decisive in contracting marriage. In this regard, the notion from Roman law is entirely true, that with regard to engagement not only is an action for entering into marriage denied but even one regarding damages or stipulated punishment, in order to keep any extraneous motivation from having an effect. But once the marriage is concluded, the ethical tie can no longer depend on sentiment. Hegel in particular gave occasion to this rationale, albeit not in accordance with his own deeper conception of marriage.[110] Besides, should one assume <151> this, then one should, marriage

---

[110]In his *Philosophy of Law* (§. 176), Hegel states: "In that marriage is firstly the immediate ethical idea, with its objective reality in the intimacy of subjective sentiment and feeling, therein lies the initial contingency of its existence. As little as any compulsion can take place regarding contracting marriage, so little does there otherwise exist a merely legal positive band that can hold the subjects together where conflicting and hostile sentiments and actions have arisen. Nevertheless, a third ethical authority is required which maintains the right of marriage, the ethical substantiality, against the mere opinion of such feeling and against the arbitrariness of mere temporary sentiment and the like, distinguishing this from total alienation and first confirming the latter and only in that case able to dissolve the marriage. Addendum: since marriage is based on *subjective arbitrary feeling*, it can be dissolved.... Marriage *ought* of course to be indissoluble, but it does not get any farther than *ought*.... Should a total alienation take place, such as through adultery, then the religious authority should permit divorce." It is

being a bond of *reciprocal love*, also recognized *unilateral alienation* as a ground of divorce, in fact as entirely permissible, entailing no disadvantage. Thus one logically proceeds from this rationale to the mutual right of arbitrary repudiation.[111] Even more than this, when feeling is decisive, no one can function as judge except the spouses themselves, and therefore only a judicial announcement of the divorce need take place, not a judicial decision. When Hegel makes the requirement of "an ethical authority which maintains the right of marriage against the contingency of mere temporary sentiment, distinguishing the latter from total alienation, and only in the case of the latter allowing the marriage to be dissolved," it must be taken into account hereby that the judge in himself has no means and no standard for these subjective feelings, but that they can only be made objectively recognizable through something like the path taken by the French civil code, to wit, through great and lasting difficulties.

Out of this mingling of feeling and will, pathological <152> and actual or ethical love, has at last emerged the complete reversal of ethical judgment as asserted by the disciples of Hegel's school in innumerable dailies and leaflets. The claim here made is that the principle followed by the church of all confessions and to this point likewise predominantly by the nations of Europe, whereby marriage, apart from the case of serious fault, is to be maintained even in the

---

precisely the opposite which follows from §. 164, however, wherein the essence of marriage is established in "consciousness gathering itself from its naturalness and subjectivity to notions of the substantial, and rather than reserving to itself contingency and arbitrariness, removing the connection to this arbitrariness and yielding to the substantial, obligating itself to the Penates."

[111] The fact that the Prussian civil code allows a childless married couple to divorce by mutual assent, while not allowing unilateral renouncement apart from injury by the guilty party, is based on the fact that in accordance with the subjective standpoint of science during that time, marriage was considered to be an arbitrary contractual relation among the spouses. Since the time of Schelling and Hegel this conception has found scarcely any scientific defender. The same is true of the motive behind this legislative determination which only now has become known through the above-cited *Representation* [n. 102]: the interest of the population. The consequences to which the Prussian code in accordance with "its private-legal principle" must lead have been laid out by Puchta *op. cit.* in the most incisive manner.

case of estrangement of minds, is itself the unethical character of legislation; ethical character, on the other hand, is when a marriage that no longer maintains what it should, is no entire unification of life, no picture of true marriage, should instead be dissolved in order to open the possibility of an ethically complete matrimonial state through another marriage. This theory does not consider that the estrangement of minds is no mere event but an act and a fault [Schuld]. It does not consider that marriage depends on every person *for himself* to make it ever more into an ethical one, should it not in its full picture answer to the ethical idea of marriage, and that only this, and this likewise imperatively, is required of him. Above all, it does not consider, and this is the headquarters of the error, that the *existing marriage* is a *higher given bond* over the spouses. For in accordance with this, all ethical demands are only viewed merely with respect to this given marriage, into which one has entered, not however the idea of marriage in general, to be totally fulfilled in this or that marriage, and that the dissolution of this marriage is quite simply the violation of an ethical bond which gains no justification through the beautiful harmony of a second connection; how harmoniously did not most of the French kings live with their mistresses! It is the same doctrine proposed by "Young Germany" without sophistry and appearance of mores: to maintain oneself bound to an existing marriage is foolishness, but where the innermost individualities have recognized themselves as belonging together, there the sexual union should, yea shall **<153>** follow, and the existing ethical bond, this priestly ceremonial, is unjustified over against it.

In accordance with the same principle to recognize no *given bond* as binding, it is the ethical demand of the father to separate from his son when he yields him worries rather than joy, to consider him totally as no longer being his son; the ethical demand of the people through uprising to separate from its king when it believes it can no longer lead a complete state life with him; the ethical demand of people to be able to separate from their bodies through suicide when these yield no satisfaction and no vigor, in fact nothing but temptations. That which is ethical is everywhere the given ethical bond recognized as being higher, standing above, while that which is unethical is that which can be dissolved arbitrarily in order to seek another, that which the person lacking strength of will and self-denial hopes to fulfill merely by virtue of natural feeling and desire. If man did not have any ethical entitlement to leave such a marriage, then it is certainly not the legislation which allows and sanctions it which is ethical, but that which does not allow such offence. The former therefore is instead based on this principle: spouses having violating the duty of marriage and ascended to a condition of hatred and irreconcilability are to be considered by the state to be a finished and immutable event (fait accompli); it grants the seal of approval; it empowers the spouses to add the highest violation to their previous violations of the marriage bond, namely to break that bond and to enter into a new marriage. Now then, as the discussion hitherto makes clear, we are far from the standpoint that legislation is always to require perfect ethical behavior of the citizen, for which reason civil laws are justified in allowing divorce in broader extension than is allowable for the mature Christian conscience. But this is ever only the exception, and that which legislation acknowledges and ought to acknowledge only as <154> a lack of perfect ethical behavior can never be passed off as its ethical principle.

Chapter 2: Concerning Mixed Marriages

§. 74. Difference of Religion

<155> *Difference of religion* must hold as a public and separative hindrance to marriage in Christian legislation. This means that no marriage between Christians and adherents of other religions (Jews, Mohamedans, pagans, members of deistic and pantheistic sects) is to exist. Not that the union of sexes among such in itself would be no true marriage, as in the case of incest. This is refuted already by the fact that when one of two non-Christian spouses becomes a Christian and the other does not, their marriage remains as valid as it was before regardless of the now-arisen difference in religion, and the church reluctantly rejects the notion of dissolution of such a marriage (**crimina in baptismo solvuntur, non conjugia**). Nevertheless, it is sin for a Christian to contract such a marriage since in marriage full religious union and mutual religious cultivation is to be sought, and the Christian who contracts such a marriage renounces this highest goal of marriage; which is why the Apostle Paul considers such a conclusion of marriage from the viewpoint that the Christian who enters into it, does so in the hope of converting the other party, and since there is no guarantee of this, he forbids it. Furthermore, it is an offence for the Christian community when such a marriage is entered into and thereby the Christian faith is treated as secondary matter. Finally it is part of the ruling authorities' concern for the public welfare not to allow marriages which are incapable <156> of fulfilling the highest, holiest purpose of marriage. On these grounds the church and the Christian state have the right and the command to prohibit such marriages and to nullify those which nevertheless have been contracted.

All of this presumes that Christianity alone is true in faith and mores, and that it is so in opposition to the other religions. From the viewpoint of the religion of reason, however, by which the things that Christianity holds in common with the other religions is the truth, and those which are particular to it are superstition, myth, and human addition, one therefore must just as consistently approve marriages among proponents of different religions, in fact even promote them in order for the immateriality of the difference among the religions to become manifest and establish itself ever more in the public consciousness. In the question regarding the permissibility of marriage between Christian and

Jew, etc., it emerges, as with the question regarding civil marriage, and even more so, that the answer only lies in the principal decision whether the Christian revelation is the truth or not, whether it is the exclusive truth or not. But the external result also confirms the truth of faith in this regard, while such marriages require not a higher unified religion but only irreligion, and the spouses in such marriages lack any power of adaptation and agreement in the succession and conflict of natural urges.

§. 75. Difference in Christian Confession

Something entirely different than the difference of religion is the difference of *confession*, marriages between Catholics and Protestants, in common parlance *mixed marriages.*[112] Here **<157>** is faith in the same revelation, the same acts of God, the same documents of the Good News; it is only the understanding of this revelation which differs, and even for this understanding the great interpretation which is contained in the three ecumenical creeds is held in common. Between Catholic and Protestant, of course, an essential divergence of religious and ethical conception exists, but no diametrical opposition as in the other case. What is common is infinitely more significant than what separates. Spouses here may be in agreement in the bond to the Redeemer, so that the highest goal of marriage need not remain unfulfilled. For this reason such a marriage cannot be considered sin as such, not simply an offence, not unconditionally a hindrance to an actual Christian marriage. On the other hand, mutual attraction and mutual satisfaction of individuality (to be distinguished from mere sensual love) is an essential aspect of marriage in accordance with God's ordinance – one marries a person and not a dogmatics – and therefore here can be of importance, where there is no absence of religious community but only a lesser degree thereof, at least for those who do not have a special external or internal vocation in the church. There are therefore examples of mixed marriage of which one can say with confidence that they were entered into according to God's will. In fact, from the standpoint that one's own confession is not the only and the perfect church and the other mere error and apostasy, one may find, albeit not commonly, a mitigation of confessional stridency and a fostering of general Christian unity.

---

[112]Compare my treatment of the issue in Harless's *Journal for Protestantism and Church* [Zeitschrift für Protestantismus und Kirche], January 1st, 1839.

This notwithstanding, it must be recognized that mixed marriages are subject to great difficulties and dangers when conducted not merely for human satisfaction but to be pleasing to God, and the above-mentioned favorable result is not <158> the rule but the exception; which moreover must become even more seldom the more the Catholic church, which of course in terms of dogma has not yet given up the Protestant church, likewise in life asserts the absolute rejection of that church to the utmost extent. And correspondingly, the intrusion of its clergy with regard to the education of children in a pitched battle rips the family apart.

Therefore, the church has neither ground nor right – the state even less so – to *declare* such marriages *null and void.*[113] The church, including the Protestant church, should however in general *advise* its members *against* them. Whether the church should be involved in such a marriage or *take part in its solemnization* is determined variously according to the standpoints of each confession, whether in fact it is simply living faith in Christ which holds as the condition of salvation or, beyond that, obedience to the determinate ecclesiastical authority derived immediately from God as well. In accordance with its strict concept, therefore, the Catholic church cannot allow participation in a truly mixed marriage and does not allow it. It makes the condition that the function of the family, the upbringing of children, is to be purely Catholic, and does not anticipate a religious bond of the Catholic part with the Protestant but instead only the guarantee of the former against such a bond. In that case it is no mixed marriage. The Protestant church on the contrary may concede a truly mixed marriage and participate in it, but even so the upbringing of children is for it the decisive thing as well.

§. 76. Upbringing of Children

<159> The religious upbringing of children can have no influence on the validity of the mixed marriage, while such a marriage can only be judged in accordance with itself and with the question of whether the spouses can remain in a religious community. But the attitude of the spouses in regard to upbringing is subject to the judgment and, as the case may be, the disciplinary action of the

[113]For the Eastern church, of course, the Irullanum declared marriage with heretics to be null and void (ἄκυρον τὸν γάμον); but the heretics here intended also stood outside the ecumenical creeds.

church at every moment in the marriage, and at the moment of the marriage's inception it is likewise a sign of what spirit the marriage will have, and the attitude of the church regarding its solemnization rightly is determined by it.[114]

The Catholic Church (in countries of mixed population) behaves towards mixed marriages, if sufficient guarantees are given for the Catholic education of children, just as it does towards purely Catholic marriages,[115] but where these guarantees are lacking, it either refuses this cooperation, or, as an extreme concession, grants it such that no approval of the Church is expressed. It allows only the passive assistance of the clergy, not the active joining and blessing, it performs the vows without mentioning the a-catholic faith of the other party in order to avoid offense, and it issues dimissorials remarking impediment to marriage on the grounds of heresy. This is the full rigor of the ecclesiastical principle, and deserves not censure but recognition.

The Protestant Church, from the strictly dogmatic (orthodox) standpoint of an earlier period, when it elevated correct dogma almost to the condition of salvation in a similar way to the Catholic Church's obedience to legitimate church authority, had to behave in a similar way, and did so.[116] But with the greater inwardness that it permanently gained during the pietistic period, it must also make the demand on the Protestant part of the family that it withhold from

---

[114] [The following paragraphs along with §§. 77–79 were not included in the first edition of this translation.]

[115] The fact that even in this case only passive assistance is granted and the marriage is to be solemnized outside the church building is only a recent and as yet still isolated arrangement, which is not even logical. For since no civil law requires the Catholic Church in any way to bring about such marriages, the alternative is only either not to solemnize them at all, or, if it does so, not to degrade a sacred act (sacrament).

[116] The Lutheran Church followed entirely the same principles as the Catholic Church, (Carpzov. jurispr. consist. lib. II. def. 6. Gerhard de conjugio §. 378. Quenstett syst. theol. pars iv. c. 14. qu. 4). The Reformed Church in France declared mixed marriages to be absolutely illicit (**illicitum**), namely it obliged the parents to warn their children, if they wished to enter into such marriages, and to lodge a protest against the marriage itself and to demonstrate this to the consistory; only if they fulfilled this obligation might they participate in the resulting marriage through endowment, etc. (la discipline des églises réformées en France chap. 13. art. 4).

none of its children the pure and certain teaching of the way of salvation as the church has recognized it; but if that Protestant part nevertheless concedes to the marriage partner of the other part the children of his or her sex, it can at least condone this and solemnize and bless the marriage itself.[117] For it permits mixed marriages not only in the (negative) view that the Protestant part is not deceived or at best wins over the Catholic part, but in the (positive) hope that even with continuing confessional difference a true Christian communion in the living inner faith, which stands above the ecclesiastical regulations, may be achieved, as it regards so many truly awakened Catholics who are nevertheless faithful to their church as its own. But it can also place this same hope in the outwardly shared education of children, that the inner power of faith will create unity. The consent of the Catholic spouse to the division can, however, be taken as a sign that this interiority has room in the marriage, and it is in this, not in the transaction over the children, that the justification lies of that indulgence in the God-ordained division of the nation itself.[118] On the other hand, if all the children are designated for the Catholic Church, this is conversely a sign that in this marriage it is precisely not the interior sense but rather the Catholic emphasis on the hierarchical union that predominates, and therein lies the most decisive expression of the contempt or even indifference of the Protestant part towards its church. Such a marriage cannot therefore be consecrated by the Protestant church, in particular while that church has emerged from a state of apathy and indifference and has become imbued once again with the profession with which it is familiar, nor allow such demeanor by its members to go unpunished. [119] Moreover, it itself assumes the responsibility if they consider the

---

[117] [The division of children according to sex was part of the legal arrangement of those times. Stahl discusses such an arrangement below, p. 136.]

[118] The fact that this consent may also have arisen out of indifferentism does not stand in the way, otherwise most purely Catholic or purely Protestant marriages could not be blessed.

[119] The sanctions of the church can only consist in exclusion from godparenthood and from ecclesiastical offices, etc., but not in exclusion from the Lord's Supper. The Protestant church can only allow this to occur for what is in itself and under all circumstances a sin against God. Only the sworn promise to alienate the children from his

renunciation of the Protestant education of their children to be permissible and harmless, just as the current recklessness of Protestant husbands has not the slightest reason or excuse[120] in the lax and indifferent behavior of the Protestant

---

church justifies exclusion of someone from the Lord's Supper, because this really is absolutely sin.

[120] Another view here is that in the case in which the Protestant party gives up nothing of what the law allows him, he is not to be blamed, and therefore the church is not to give any sign of disapproval but is to consecrate the marriage. Accordingly, in Prussia, for example, and elsewhere where the same law applies, it would have to be insisted that the Protestant bridegroom should not withdraw any of his children from the Protestant church, otherwise he should be denied the blessing, whereas the Protestant bride should not be asked to do anything at all, and should be granted the blessing regardless of the fact that she alienates her entire offspring from the church, unless she expressly promises what already applies according to the law. This view does not seem tenable to me. The church cannot make its demands on its members according to chance, whether the civil laws determine things one way or another; that is not the religious standard of marriage. This would mean that the Protestant Church in a country in which it is marginalized and the children of mixed marriages all become Catholic, would nevertheless have to approve of these marriages and cooperate for them. But it also leads to a double grievance under equal legislation such as that of Prussia. On the one hand, if the church does not address all children unconditionally like the Catholic Church does, it is unjust to proceed against the Protestant bridegroom who believes he must encumber his bride with the children of her sex. On the other hand, the Protestant bride who enters into a mixed marriage under such a law is not free from the accusation of indifference to her church if she has not somehow assured herself of her bridegroom's intentions, and would thereby be strengthened in such indifference. That the woman, as the serving part, has no responsibility, would be an oriental and pre-Christian idea, and according to it she should also have no responsibility in those countries where the laws determine the division according to sex, if she leaves the religion of all children to the man. The church can only have an autonomous standard, independent of civil legislation. Either it must insist on all children everywhere, as was the older strict practice, or it will see to the relinquishment of children of the opposite sex. There is no third option. Only the former strictness is completely consistent. But even the latter leniency has a principle,

Church itself. It goes without saying that in a matter that depends so much on the innermost state of the souls of the personalities involved, both pastoral and ecclesiastical-disciplinary behavior must be adapted with great freedom and breadth to the considerations of the particular case.

§. 77. Contracts Regarding Religious Upbringing

It is proper for the church to make *contracts* for the future education of children a condition of its cooperation, where the civil laws attach judicial effect to such contracts; for to the church they are then as much as an immediate grant of rights over the children. But if this effect is not attached to the contracts, they give no security against changed convictions, and it is objectionable to impose on the legal conscience of the promisor what ought to be against his religious conscience. The church then has no other unimpeachable means than to carefully investigate the *present* disposition and intention of the betrothed, and to demand declarations on this from both parts, which are then only of an assertory, not promissory nature, in which it therefore imposes on the other part only present veracity, but not future action against present conviction.

Under all circumstances, however, it is reprehensible for the church of the other part to demand or accept an *oath-bound promise* that the education of the children into its faith will be permitted or even left unhindered. Such an oath is a sin for the one who swears it as well as for the one who demands it. For even if the person swearing has no conscience at present about allowing his children to be brought up in a creed other than his own, the positive truth of which is in any case not certain to him, since he does not himself convert to it, he

---

it is a completely different kind of Catholicism, to which the Protestant part joins, depending on whether the Catholic part agrees to the division or not. The attachment to the respective civil legislation has neither principle nor consequence. The result that, if the religion of the father is decisive everywhere, parity will emerge on the whole, may only be a subordinate consideration. The concern of the church is not primarily the overall result for the expansion of its domain, but the particular marriage, and in this the first thing is the Protestant husband, his dutiful behavior and the securing of his salvation, and only afterward the children to be expected in the future.

The civil legislation is not violated or thwarted by the procedure of the church recommended here, since where one church refuses cooperation, the other certainly grants it.

nevertheless necessarily lives in uncertainty and in his own awareness of uncertainty as to whether or not he will have a conscience about it in the future. But it is indisputably sacrilege and sin to promise on oath that of which one is and must be doubtful as to whether it is lawful in his time to do it, to take God as surety for that which one may recognize as contrary to his commandment. If the Catholic swears to make his children Catholic, and the Protestant to make them Protestant, this is only an affirmation on oath of a recognized duty. But if the Catholic swears to let his children become Protestants, and vice versa, or the Jew swears to let his children become Christians, he swears by God to do what he is not allowed to do according to his belief in God, and therefore commits a sin by the oath itself, apart from its fulfillment or non-fulfillment. This does not change even if the church to which the oath is made really is the true God-ordained church. For the oath depends not only on the nature of the matter, but also on the consciousness of the person swearing. Whoever swears assertorically to a true fact, but in the opinion that it is false or in doubt about it, commits perjury. In the same way, anyone who promises his children on oath to the true church when he himself does not believe in its truth is committing perjury. What does not come from faith is sin. Now, should it not be a sin to swear one's children to a church when one's own confession is contrary to it? For the same reason such an oath, if it has really been taken, is not binding; for the oath against one's own duty is not binding according to a principle that is undisputed in the church,[121] and the church to which the person swearing belongs is authorized and called upon to declare it void.

§. 78. The State and Recognition of Mixed Marriages

The state has no reason to promote mixed marriages, since religious indifferentism also shakes its foundation, but it does have an interest, in a mixed population, in the existence of the possibility of intermarriage, as a condition of uniform patriotic sentiment; it must therefore secure this possibility if a church ever wished to frustrate it for its own purpose (e.g. by refusing to grant dimissorials).

The following principle applies to the right of the state against the church in this respect: it can demand everything from the church that the church does not regard as contrary to God's commandment (**divina institutio**) according to its

---

[121] C. 22. qu. 4. – C. 2. 33. X. de jurejur.

own doctrine and practice, even if it would like to refuse such by virtue of merely human ecclesiastical considerations (see above pp. 97f.).

Thus the state can absolutely demand from the Roman Catholic Church passive assistance, proclamation and dimissorialia in the forms customary for this case, and the omission of censures. For it is clear from its own practice that it can grant all this without violating divine order, and if it does so in some places (e. g. for Bavaria in the instructional letter **litteris jam inde** 1834) only in the event of the threat of even greater evil and offense to the "detriment of religion" (that is, the conversion of the Catholic part), hence in its interest, the state can demand that it grant such unconditionally, out of respect for civil order and out of consideration for the state, which gives it protection and care and public authority, and which is concerned with keeping the peace between the confessions. The state can also prohibit one church from making contractual promises to the members of the other and binding them contrary to the commandments of their church, but it would be more advisable for it not to concern itself with this and only to reject the legal effectiveness of such promises. But the state cannot and should not allow one church to accept such promises from the members of the other *under oath*, and it is entitled to punish this through penalties imposed on the clergy, since it has the right and duty to prevent the seduction of its subjects into acts that are immoral and sinful under all circumstances.

On the other hand, the state is not entitled to impose on the Catholic Church any act of approval and ecclesiastical consecration for such marriages, such as the blessing, the dimissorialia without mention of the impediment, or the blessing of the woman who has given birth. Nor can it forbid the most precise investigation of the present intention with regard to the upbringing of the child, both with regard to its member ("bridal examination") and with regard to the other party.

§. 79. Principles of State Recognition

For its own (civil) regulations on the religious upbringing of children from mixed marriages, the state must observe the following principles if (as in Germany) the confessions have equal rights:

1. *The concordant will and joint disposition of the two spouses* must first and foremost determine the religion of the children at every moment until they become independent. A legal provision which determines the religion of the children even against the common will of the parents would be contrary to the right

of the parents, but it would also be contrary to the religious promotion of the children, since the question as to which of the two spouses predominates in the religious sense, and to which confession the particular marriage as a whole leans, is so decisive for this. The church, however, has no right to oppose this. For the church has no direct right to the children against the educational authority of the parents, but only a right to the parents belonging to it, that they bring their children to it. This right must, however, be protected by the state for the publicly recognized church; if both parents belong to the same church, the state may not allow them to alienate their children from it, for example, by letting Roman Catholic parents allow their children to become German-Catholic. Only in the case of mixed marriages does this right of the two churches cancel each other out; for parental authority, which is always an inseparable whole, here stands under neither confession entirely.

2. On the other hand, *contracts between parents* concerning the religion of their children, i.e., promises which are binding for the future, even if one party has in the meantime changed his mind, must be declared inadmissible and invalid. The religion and religious upbringing of children is not the subject of a contract, it is not something disposable; it is an ethical duty and profession, and cannot be disposed of or contracted over. Parents always remain subject to the dictates of their conscience and cannot pretend to disregard such at any time when it becomes clear to them. As little as one can make a contract about one's own religion, just as little can one make a contract about that of one's children.

The legal arrangement itself – which thus occurs if and insofar as the spouses do not jointly decide otherwise – can be either that the children follow the father or that they are divided according to sex. In favor of the former is the natural and legal principle of paternal authority and the preference for uniformity of religious upbringing. In favor of the latter is the fact that, according to the Christian position, the woman nevertheless retains her independent personality under the authority of the man, which is why in the decision on the means of religious and moral education she must be subordinate to him everywhere, but in the decision on the highest end itself, on the choice of religion, she should not be excluded; furthermore, that if all the children follow the father, the mother occupies an isolated, alienated position in the family likewise for her person; finally, that since the permission of mixed marriage rests in general on the hope of a reconciliation of the confessional opposition between the spouses through intimate religiousness and family love, this very reconciliation must also be possible between the children with different religious upbringing, while on the other hand the awareness of this opposition is stimulated in the children even without this, through the mother's differing religion.

Both arrangements are therefore permissible, and it cannot be said of either of them that it is the appropriate one and that the other is not. Such an unconditional judgment is not possible here for two reasons: First, because the mixed marriage always remains an inharmonious relationship, and for this reason a harmonious solution of it is not possible everywhere, but rather, according to one side or the other, disagreements must always arise; second, because the legal arrangement in this case should only ever be subsidiary, if the spouses do not decide otherwise according to their particular confessional temperature, and there are no fundamentally unconditional necessities for merely subsidiary arrangements. In the case of an irenic position of the churches themselves, the division according to sex is certainly the more appropriate, but the more sharply opposition and polemics emerge, the more it will come to pass that every mixed marriage must throw itself completely and unconditionally into the arms of one church, in which case the provision that this is subsidiary to that of the man will prove its worth. But the result will then be that only the man's church will be involved, and that the woman herself will often follow suit. In short, given the severe opposition of the churches, mixed marriage is in fact no longer possible, and every mixed marriage will merge into an unmixed one.

Chapter 3: Paternal Power

§. 80. The Purpose of the Parent-Child Relationship

<161> The purpose (τέλος) of relationships between parents and children is the upbringing of the latter into full human existence, into spiritual and civil independence; no less as well, however, is this purpose the satisfaction for the parents to have a natural bond and attachment to their children; and eventually, beyond upbringing, the enduring bond of love and piety, respectively, for each.

§. 81. The Nature of Paternal Power

Until the child achieves independence, the relationship has an organic activity, that is, a continuous action (function), which differs for each member, focusing on one and the same goal, namely this self-same independence. This goal entails on the one hand parental duties: alimentation, education in accordance with station, daughter's trousseau, and the like, and on the other hand parental rights. The latter are firstly *protection and representation* outwardly, in particular in court (the Germanic *mundium)*, then the *power of upbringing*. These together are the concept of *paternal power*. The power of upbringing extends across all relations of life: choice of calling, religion, marriage. To what degree children have a choice in these areas differs according to the object and the age of the children. The power of upbringing certainly has as one of its <162> essential aspects the furthering of the child towards attaining the goal, although as the entire bond is also to serve the satisfaction of the parents, so does it no less include a rule over the children for their own benefit, namely disposal over their services and labors.

This thought, grounded in the essence of the matter, certainly also underlay Roman paternal power, although in line with the spirit of the whole Roman law it is the right of the father as such which forms the leading principle of legal formation and not the protection and upbringing of children, for which in the final analysis this right chiefly exists. For this reason guardianship, the main aspect of which is protection, had no analogy in Roman law, while according to Germanic law paternal authority and guardianship are entirely homogeneous (Rudorff).

§. 82. The Duration of Paternal Power

Paternal power ends with the independence of the child, which is its main goal. For this, however, full independence is required, to wit, both inner spiritual independence, i.e., maturity (coming of age), and external civil independence, i.e., the ability to maintain oneself (one's own household). This is emancipation according to German law. Roman emancipation is not suitable to the twofold perspective of the purpose of paternal power, in that in itself this power lasts a lifetime, and in that it can be dissolved through caprice prior to the attainment of independence.

The organic action of the bond ends with the independence of the child, but the ethical bond of love and piety continues to exist.[122] This generates not only moral claims but also **<163>** legal ones, albeit, in accordance with the general character of law (Book II [*Principles of Law*], §. 6), only of a negative content. This includes the hindrance of certain disrespectful or uncharitable actions (for example legal charges, incriminating testimony, etc.), the obligation to mutual alimentation in extreme need, and the like. Mostly, however, this bond expresses itself in *the law of succession*.

§. 83. Concerning the Property* of Children

A similar principle as with that of spouses holds with regard to the property* of children. As long as the paternal power lasts, and so the children have their existence dependently simply in the family, then their property* as well, should they have any, should serve the family just as do their personal performances, in that they resort under the administration and usufruct of the father. But this restriction ends with attained independence (emancipation), and with respect to this they at that point should already be capable of acquiring separate property*. Neither the ancient Roman incapacity of children to acquire nor the later Roman-legal ongoing partial usufruct of the father even after emancipation are appropriate.

---

[122] This is the deeper meaning of the Attic institution that the paternal power lasts for life but that the son actually becomes independent at the age of twenty, by being entered in the civil register. The latter in Athens depended on political maturity, as in Germanic law it depended on private-legal maturity.

§. 84. Concerning Adoption

A lack of children on the one side and a lack of means for upbringing and of an estate on the other leads to artificial reproduction, that strangers enter in the relation of physical parents – *adoption*. It is the substitute for the parental bond. The Romans one-sidedly treated it as a means for parental <164> power, even though it is the latter which is a means. It therefore ought not exceed the requirement of such a substitute, to wit, it is permissible only to the childless, and the natural bond is not be dissolved.[123]

§. 85. The Natural-Law Explanation of the Parent-Child Relationship

This relationship confronted the older natural law theory most peculiarly with the difficulty, in fact the impossibility, of deducing it as legally binding, it definitely being given by nature and not grounded by human will, thus ruling out the application of the presumed contract, this school's ever-ready way out of difficulty. Therefore already Grotius[124] found that in strictness it should not be accounted among legal relationships, while Thomasius in his later separation of law and morality decisively and logically ascribed the relationship between parents and children simply to the latter.[125] Kant[126] attempted to derive the legal nature of this relation from the fact that, because one brings a person arbitrarily into existence without his consent (!), one is also legally obligated to provide conditions satisfying to him. Should one agree with this line of argumentation, then parents would be obliged to provide alimentation and the like while children would not be obliged to submit to parental authority in case they were more content without it.

§. 86. Concerning Guardianship and the Servant Relationship

<165> *Guardianship* is a substitute for paternal power. It therefore naturally entails protection and upbringing. The power of upbringing is here lesser, in that with respect to the preference for the natural bond the share of the mother

---

[123] Regarding the obligations stemming from paternity out of wedlock, see my *Parliamentary Speeches*, January 17th and February 4th 1854.

[124] *De Jure Belli*, Book II, ch. 7, §. 4.

[125] *Institutions of Divine Jurisprudence*, Book III, ch. 4.

[126] *Doctrine of Law*, pp. 113, 114.

expands, and even the inclination of the already mature child (e.g., to enter into a vocation) has more weight for a guardian than a father. Protection on the other hand is more significant in that the inherited property* is the chief consideration. On the whole, the position of the guardian is less a right, like the father's, than a function, and in the end terminates in mere claims to property*. Guardianship is however for that reason by no means a mere requirement of *administration* (**negotiorum gestio**). Apart from any personal and educational influence on the ward, the necessity that the ward must recognize this administration and representation is in itself a bond of enduring personal dependence which is foreign to claims-relations. Should one rather wish to consider guardianship as a public office, there is no grounds to dispute this. It would be more in accordance with nature, however, to consider it as a familial bond, at least in our legal condition, where the guardian also participates in upbringing, and therefore the relationship in terms of its content supplies everything that nature made the task of the familial, i.e., the paternal power.

Just so is the servant relationship a sort of family relationship and no mere obligation of contracted service (**locatio operarum**). For it does not concern individual isolated services but a continuum of them, having as substrate a certain life community, a household community. For this reason it has the aspect of domestic power over and above that of obligated contracted service. Hence the servant (according to our law) stands in his entire conduct of life in a certain dependence upon mastership, and the latter in a certain responsibility [Haftung] for the ser- **<166>** vant, and there are e.g. many remarks which in other contexts could be construed as injurious but which regarding servants are not treated as such. Such dependence upon a strange family, to which one does not belong as an actual member through the unity of blood, is of course a relation that does not correspond to the prototype of the fulfilled human condition. Nevertheless, it is simply ineradicably grounded in earthly conditions (Book I [*Philosophical Foundations*], §. 46) just as is the distinction between wealth and poverty, from which it in the final analysis is derived. It therefore is not eliminated when one ignores it, i.e., when it is conceived not as a dependency but as a contract relation, so that when the agreed performances take place the servant stands on a fully equal level with the master. For in fact the dependency nevertheless remains since the servant in need of food must ultimately submit to the master, and the only disadvantage is that both parties regard each other only as a means for their convenience and their preservation, who are inwardly committed to nothing but what has been promised. In this manner mastership is arranged badly, while even worse, the servant is abandoned. The latter is furthermore exposed to greater temptation of immorality which inheres in a lesser, in itself unelevated status, by virtue of the greater license stemming from the dissolution of the bond. The ennobling of this relation does not consist in its being dissolved into a mere claim relation but in its approximation to the familial bond. This can only be accomplished through custom, not legislation; but the latter at least ought not destroy the precondition of such custom, which is the legal recognition of domestic power and responsibility. On the other hand, the stricter boundaries of domestic power, the supervision of its use by the ruling authorities, and the complete freedom to dissolve the bond are the guarantees of the personal freedom of the servant, which recent times of course **<167>** did not discover but, rightly, have asserted more strictly.

Chapter 4: Freedom of Instruction

§. 87. The Right of Fathers and the State in Instruction

<169> It is the right of the father and the core of paternal power (§. 81) to determine the upbringing and instruction of children. The state cannot remove this right and usurp it. But for its part the state has a vocation and right to direct [leiten] upbringing and instruction. The upbringing and instruction of the children is incumbent upon the father; but it is incumbent on the state to ensure pure mores and higher intellectual culture [Bildung] for the nation. Therefore upbringing and instruction are the outgrowth of both paternal power and state power, the former for individual upbringing, the latter for national education. In particular, however, to the degree that it concerns training for public office, the setting of conditions and thus the regulation of instruction are an affair of state.

Accordingly, the state has the right:

1. Generally to require a certain degree of education [Bildung] – elementary instruction – and to this end to prescribe that all children either attend the popular school or receive an education equal to the popular school.

2. Of all who maintain schools or otherwise wish to undertake instruction as gainful employment – not merely as tutor in support of a single head of household –to require above all certain moral guarantees, then also certain public tests and certificates of ability as to whether they meet that general <170> standard of popular instruction.

3. To require attendance at public institutions (gymnasia, universities) for state offices and in order to practice as physician, lawyer, etc.

This has been the customary arrangement up until the most recent times, and is so even to this day.

§. 88. The Contemporary Demand for Freedom of Instruction

This arrangement is now opposed by the demand for *freedom of instruction.* By this is intended *firstly* that anyone, regardless of any examination or authorization, is allowed to impart instruction and to set up an educational institution, and therefore that anyone is allowed to run such an institution; *secondly,* that only *a final examination* be required of state offices and practice as attorney or physician, not attendance at any public institution, that, as the saying goes, the state only inquire after the knowledge, not after the source of the knowledge.

In Belgium this freedom of instruction has been fundamentally and fully realized.[127] It has thus become the poster image for the same. In France in the final years of the July monarchy, it was vigorously demanded (by the Catholic party) (since it was also promised there in the constitution). It was claimed here as an inalienable right on the basis of the title of individual freedom, and mainly the title of paternal power, in that only the father can decide to whom he entrusts his children. But the demand for freedom of instruction in fact is not justified, and least of all for these titles.

The right of each and every father to determine the instruction and upbringing of his children does not preclude the state from exercising the right to protect the entire population from teachers without ability or moral guarantees, as little as does the right of every man to decide about his body preclude the state from prohibiting quacks from practicing medicine. The specific decision therein always remains with the father, but the state circumscribes the circumference by excluding that which, in terms of the public consideration, is impermissible. The **<171>** comparison made in the debates that the state should not apply preventive measures to instruction as little as it does to the press, and only intervene when a school gives offense, does not apply. For even admitting the absolute

[127] Article 17 of the Belgian Charter states: "l'enseignement est libre, touts mesure préventive est interdite, la répression des délits n'est réglée que par la loi" [teaching is free, all preventive measures are prohibited, the repression of offenses is regulated only by law]. According to Belgian legislation, practice as a lawyer or doctor is conditional on the scientific degree of doctor or licentiate, but all degrees for philosophy, letters, law and medicine depend only on an examination, not on study at an institution. The law of higher education determines "toute personne peut se présenter aux examens et obtenir des grades sans distinction du temps, du lieu ou de la manière dont elle a fait ses études" [anyone can take the exams and obtain grades regardless of time, place or how they studied]. This examination is not consigned to a state school even for obtaining degrees, so that there is no indirect obligation to attend, but special examination commissions are set up as juries (in Brussels) for this purpose. Each of them is composed of seven persons, two of whom are designated by the Chamber of Deputies, two by the Senate (upper house) and three by the government.

impermissibility of preventive measures for the press, the press remains the activity and vocation of individuals even when acting in the public square; by contrast, the education and instruction of the nation is an activity and vocation of the state itself. Even though in ancient states they were the exclusive vocation of the state, and even though nowadays, in the spirit of the Christian-German peoples, the first place in this comes to the father, that vocation of the state is still not entirely absorbed.

Above all, the right of individual freedom cannot be asserted against the requirement of attendance at specified educational institutions as a precondition for civil service on the grounds that the provenance of knowledge is of no concern to the state. For although with regard to specific individuals, each considered in his own right, the place at which he obtained his knowledge may be a matter of indifference, it is not so with regard to the level of education of the applicants taken collectively. This collective result depends upon the educational institutions. The mere final examination is no substitute for attendance there, since the standard for all examinations must necessarily be established in accordance with the candidates themselves, and the general avoidance of truly appropriate public educational institutions would therefore lower the standard itself, which it is the concern of the state to maintain at its level. To what degree freedom here recommends itself on educational grounds is an entirely different question; it cannot be required on legal grounds.

Freedom of education in this rationale is just as revolu- <172> tionary as the declaration of the rights of man. It destroys higher order and leading in favor of unlimited freedom of individuals; in its consequences it leads to the state having to tolerate even God-denying institutions of instruction, in the same way that it cannot do anything about a God-denying tutor.

§. 89. Religion and Freedom of Instruction

The deeper motivation from which the demand for freedom of instruction has sprung is however by no means individual freedom or the inviolability of the paternal power but instead the effort to detach education from the state and turn it over to the clergy. This undoubtedly was the intent and apparently the result of freedom of instruction in Belgium. It was likewise the sole object of the desire for it in France. Through this freedom the effort was made for the clergy and the orders to be able to open schools for elementary and gymnasial instruction apart from any interference by the state, and for attendance in these schools not to be disadvantageous in future application for civil office, so that Catholics might send their children to these schools without hindrance. In a word, what was desired was *ecclesiastical popular instruction in emancipation from the state.*

There is much stronger basis in truth in this real motivation than in that asserted one. The *religious conscience of the father* and the *vocation to instruct of the church* have their well-founded right vis-à-vis the state, and the appeal to this ground is a great deal more proper than to that of the right of individual freedom and paternal power. The state has the right to have every father subordinate his view regarding the method of upbringing and instruction and regarding the ability of specific teachers to the goal of national instruction; but it has no right to have the father subordinate his religious faith itself to that goal. <173> Such exclusive and unrestricted power of the state over education is something out of the ancient world, and the deeper life of the Germanic peoples opposes this, as do the divine commands of the Christian faith which stand elevated over the state. No less does the state-recognized church have a right to a share of popular instruction. Certainly, it is not its right either directly or indirectly, through the freedom of the head of household, to direct instruction and the institutions established for it, to determine the standard and form of intellectual cultivation. It does have the right to have an effect on the institutions of learning to the degree that the students do not become alienated from it but rather become more closely connected to it. For institutions of learning are also of necessity institutions of upbringing; every lesson educates, and the system of teaching to which students are subjected cannot be without influence on their religious sentiment. This is not restricted to religious instruction; other studies, e.g., in history and natural science, exert a religious influence; that influence is exerted mostly by the personality of the teacher. Therefore, when the state school is dechristianized or set into opposition with the relevant recognized confession, then its monopoly or authoritative power is no longer justified, neither in direct manner in the state school, nor even in indirect manner in the institutions of education for state offices. For in that case the law of conscience is in effect; one cannot coerce a father to submit his child to an influence antagonistic to his religion, and the right of the church to conduct its educational vocation separated from the state is no less valid.

By contrast, it is a transgression when the church fundamentally and therefore generally (or at least where divergences with the state power exist, which can never be entirely removed) calls for national education on its own, separated and even emancipated from the state, as, e.g., in Germany where freedom of <174> education is demanded more openly and consistently, not in general but only for the church, that the episcopal people's or secondary schools not be supervised by the state, that examinations of teachers not be required for them, since the church itself provides the moral and scientific guarantees here. Education as such, the cultivation of intelligence and knowledge, is not however the vocation of the church but of the state, and even upbringing, the cultivation of sentiment [Gesinnung], has an aspect which the state cannot leave to the church alone. A care is entrusted to the state for the sake of loyalty and national patriotism, and for recognition of civil considerations and peace among the confessions, which the church could not possibly provide; and by no means does education by the church in itself offer the guarantee that it will not establish a sentiment in which those duties appear, not independent and unconditional, but subordinated to the power and disposition of the ecclesiastical authority, the guarantee, thus, that it will not instill the principles of Boniface VIII and Bellarmine.[128]

The task is therefore to maintain the school on the Christian and, depending on circumstances, the specific confessional foundations, and to accord the church the fullest, most effective share in this, without giving up the solid grip of the state for positive guidance of instruction and the supervision of religious influences. No objection of oppressed conscience and no pursuit of emancipation which opposes this is grounded. When however the state establishes a system of education detached from or even in contradiction to the religious-ecclesiastical foundations, there it is well-grounded, according to the degree of contradiction, to assert the inde- <175> pendence of the religious conscience of the father and the educational vocation of the church, right up to the demand for freedom of instruction.

---

[128]See my lectures on *Protestantism as a Political Principle*, p. 51, and *Catholic Refutations*, a statement accompanying the fourth edition thereof, p. 19.

Chapter 5: Inheritance

§. 90. Significance of the Right of Succession

<177> The law of succession is a consequence of the family bond, in particular the parental bond. The latter has by nature the purpose (τέλος) of imparting the fullness of existence and therefore also satisfaction to the children, and in them to have the furtherance of one's own personality and therefore also of property*. It is only because of the children that the right of succession even exists, even when it is extended to other natural relations.

In accordance with this – its natural goal as the furtherance of personality – inheritance is not an immediate admission (acquisition of property) to the *objects* of property*, arising from grounds of the law of property*, but by means of a bond among the persons, admission to the entire *sphere* of property* *rights* of the testator. The total content of this sphere (rights and liabilities [Verbindlichkeiten]) therefore retains its relation continuously to the testator and thereby its juristic unity (**successio universalis**), a unity which precedes that of the individual objects, not one which, as with the **universitas facti**, first arises with their accumulation, and thus also is valid even where only one object ("**res licet minima**") is extant.[129]<178>

For the entire human race, however, the *order* and *continuity* by which it holds property* in the succession of generations lies in this familial succession (and the testamentary succession which imitates it), by means of which it uninterruptedly governs property* as the substrate of consciousness and will and preserves both the legal spheres of persons respecting property* and, through these, the continuity of the generations.

---

[129]German succession as well, although rightly characterized as **successio singularis** vis-à-vis Roman succession, is not this in the strictest sense; since entry into the inheritance occurs only via a connection to the testator (whether the first acquirer or the last possessor is irrelevant here), not directly (as e.g. in the case of purchase); and insofar as the heir is not liable to creditors of the testator, namely regarding the inherited immovable property [Gut], this is not because he is a singular successor but because the testator could not encumber the immovable property with debt.

§. 91. Forms of Succession

Accordingly, the succession of children – and, by analogy, relatives in general – on the one hand is the necessary consequence of the familial bond, the purpose inherent in parental property* itself. But according to the *self-causation of the person,* particularly with respect to property, which the parents do not lose, it presents itself on the other hand as *the consequence of the act of the parents*, as a gift and impartation, albeit therefore as a *duty* of parents in this respect as well. Hence it is not an "admission to the particular possession of in-itself common property*,"[130] as if the right already previously existed and the other recipients or exercisers had been removed, but is truly succession, the new acquisition of a propertied estate [eines Vermögens], and therefore on the one hand determined by the will of the parents, as will be shown presently, and on the other hand dependent upon the will of the children (right of acceptance or **<179>** renunciation).

To this aspect is joined the freedom of disposition of the testator – *testamentary succession.*

When, that is, succession is likewise a consequence of the testator's act, then he is also entitled in greater or lesser degree to specify it in terms of content. Hence he may:

1. give to his natural heirs by means of a special declaration of will that which was already due them by virtue of the bond, in doing so declaring it outwardly and publicly as a work of his will,

2. more closely determine in detail this legally necessary succession, e.g., arrangement regarding inheritance portions,

3. impose legacies and other obligations on the heirs (the legacies are valid not by virtue of a disposal over the objects of property*, since the testator does not have this, but by virtue of the family-like power over the heirs, for which reason: where there is no heir, there is no legacy),

4. disinherit them for debt (this as well is only the consequence of the fact that succession is a work of the act of the testator; were however succession only

---

[130] Hegel, *Philosophy of Law*, §. 178. This expression is too broad regardless of the truth of the thought Hegel thereby intends to express. It is applicable at best to the **successio ex pacto et providentia majorum**, and even in this case one inherits not from the last possessor but from the first acquirer, and it is upon that act that the succession rests.

"admission to in-itself common property*," then disinheritance would be impermissible even with the most extreme debt, as little as it is permissible for the father to punish the children by taking *their* property),

5. finally, bequeath the estate purely in accordance with his own will, construct entirely artificial bonds of inheritance, be it for the entire estate where no natural necessity exists, be it only for a portion of the same. <180>

§. 92. Testate Succession

Accordingly, the inner purpose of parental property*, viz., to be left to the children, is the only ground not merely of the remaining intestate succession but also of testamentary succession. There would be no testament without intestate succession, the former being partly the more specific determination, partly the surrogate, of the latter. The character of the testament is therefore not free disposition over property, since this ought not extend beyond life, but the free imitation of the natural familial bond, analogous to adoption.[131]

Testamentary succession therefore is restricted by natural limitations, particularly in the children; it can only be implemented to the degree that these do not exist or are not excessively restricted.

The right of the last will and testament was not entirely lacking with any people but rather occupied an extremely secondary position after the right of intestate heirs, in particular the children; so e.g. in Attic law, which did not authorize a testament where no children existed. Roman law first brought testamentary freedom to decisive and independent, not mere subsidiary, validity, but to the degree that it violated the natural bonds, to wit, bound to legal forms but unrestricted in terms of content. Later development moderated this, in particular through the **querela inofficiosi** borrowed from the Greeks, and the principle of an obligatory portion. The latter is still too slight in Roman law, to wit, measuring a third to a half. The Prussian civil code rightly sets this amount higher, while beyond that the French <181> code guarantees the children half to three-fourths of what would be their intestate portion.

---

[131]This is demonstrated most clearly in the Attic law, which knows no other form of bequeathal to **extraneos** than through adoption by means of testament, so that the testament must necessarily include the adoption of the heir. See Gans, *Universal-Historical Development of the Law of Succession* [universalhistor. Entwickelung des Erbrechts], I, p. 315.

§. 93. Intestate Succession

Because the bond between parents and children is the origin of all right of intestate succession, the solidarity of those descending from one procreator is the natural principle of the *order of succession* with him and among themselves. Accordingly, the Germanic *parentela principle* appears to be the natural and intimate one before mere proximity of degree, although in the same clan [Sippe] this would be the Roman *principle of representation*.

Regarding intestate succession the viewpoint has ruled from earliest times that the estate [Vermögen] remains within the male line as the superior sex. As such, in Athens the complete exclusion of daughters alongside sons and the institution of the epikleros,[132] in Rome the exclusion, not of course of the daughter, but of those descending from the daughters (the cognates), and the Germanic preference for the male line in the succession to the patrimony. Since through Christianity, however, the female sex has been elevated to an essentially equal position, it is in general owed the same entitlement, in the way that later Ro- **<182>** man law developed it. Only regarding landed property, particularly the landed nobility where such exists, is a preference for the male line justifiable in respect to the civil and political position of the family which it includes and which is represented by that property. Here therefore the female line is maintained by the male: through the agnates, the husband, the jointure. On the other hand, if the estate comprises movables, the female sex would have no security against poor administration by the male sex given such an arrangement. Additionally, that arrangement assumes that marriages largely are concluded within the same station. It is from the civil and political significance of landed property

---

[132]["*epikleros* (fem. adj. acting as noun), *epiklerote* (abstract noun): An *epikleros* was the daughter of a man who died leaving no male heir; she was not his heiress, but possession of his estate went together with her hand in marriage." S. C. Todd, selections by Michael de Brauw, "A Glossary of Athenian Legal Terms," in Adriaan Lanni, ed., "Athenian Law in its Democratic Context" (*Center for Hellenic Studies On-line Discussion Series*). Republished in C.W. Blackwell, ed., *Dēmos: Classical Athenian Democracy* (A. Mahoney and R. Scaife, edd., *The Stoa: a consortium for electronic publication in the humanities* [www.stoa.org]), edition of March 16, 2003. Contact: cwb@stoa.org.]

that the institution of inalienability and beyond that of indivisibility spring. This can be treated appropriately in the doctrine of the estates [Ständen].[133]

§. 94. Recognition of Inheritance

Since inheritance is an expression of the familial bond, in fact to that degree is itself the familial bond expressing itself in the working of property*, not only is its recognition essential by the individuals from whom one wishes the factual performance, but a general public recognition of the heir as well. Just as fatherhood or marriage naturally cannot be recognized by one disputant and denied by another but must either exist in the same way for everyone or not, so also inheritance (§. 63). The Athenian institution is based on such a notion: if an inheritance was to be settled, everyone with a claim came before the Archon, who ascertained the heirs among them, and when they were recognized, it was <183> public, in front of all. By contrast, the Romans allowed the inheritance to be fought over among the disputants in isolation, and in the various proceedings which in this manner arose the judges chanced to come to various decisions, with one-half of a testament remaining in force, the other half overturned, producing intestate succession. This is an abuse. The Roman institution nevertheless is based on the no-less true concept that the right of inheritance ought not be ascertained by the ruling authorities (administratively) but must remain open to every claimant for legal action. Even so, the two notions are in no way irreconcilable.

Furthermore, the action regarding inheritance is not to be considered a mere **actio in rem**, i.e., a suit against the totality of property [Sachen], but analogously to family actions, as a **praejudicium** which nevertheless likewise contains its realization in individual performances and restitutions. Considered in this light, the entire treatment is quite simple; the matter initially present itself in this manner to an impartial person, while the Roman jurists' conception of the action as a mere **actio in rem** leads to the unnatural expression that one must consider the **debitor hereditarius** to be a **quasi juris possessor** and the like. A double component, the right to the **successio** and the right to the **hereditas**,

[133]The Mosaic law, which exists here as everywhere as a divine prototype, does not establish indivisibility and the exclusion of the later-born, but does establish by means of the Jubilee year the inalienability and maintenance of landed property in the same family, which otherwise can naturally only be determined according to the male line.

accordingly cannot be distinguished. Instead, although the inheritance is precisely a bond for the sake of the propertied estate [das Vermögen], the manifold effects are given in itself, which are united by it as its cause. In technical treatment, therefore, one ever only has to apply the principle: when the bond is recognized by the opposing party or by means of evidence is forced to do so,[134] and he <184> himself cannot find support in a special right, then everything that was the testator's must become the plaintiff's: his real rights, his claims, *but also his factual advantages*, to the degree that they have a legal relation and were lost through the inheritance, e.g., the possession of a thing which the testator detained merely as **depositum**. All of this must be able to be achieved through the action of inheritance, since all of this is only the consequence of recognizing the bond of succession. Should one consider it as an **actio in rem**, then the inclusion of such a merely detained thing cannot be justified, while on the contrary it is entirely natural when considered as a **praejudicium**; for the thing belongs together with the estate of the testator in the broadest sense, it belongs to his pecuniary situation, and therefore must also become the representative of his person. Through the inclusion of such things in the whole, the heir in no way receives more property* than the testator had, he only receives *ways of pursuing his rights* which the testator did not have; and this is appropriate and necessary, since he must factually first obtain possession of the property* that the testator already had. If this is considered to be peculiar, then it must be considered so above all because the heir had the **hereditas petitio** at all, to which not even the testator himself was entitled.

§. 95. Natural-Law Theory of Succession

Earlier natural-law theory conceived of testamentary succession as the product of property, thus the completely free disposition of the testator over what belongs to him, with intestate succession viewed as a presumptive testament. So Grotius[135] and all his followers, and likewise the civilians up <185> until most recent times. Just so on the other hand did Kant conceive of succession as

---

[134]Throughout nearly the entire history of literature one considered it noteworthy that the action of inheritance also runs against the **pro possessore** possessor; but were it not admissible here, then it could not hold against the **pro herede** possessor, in that the latter is a **pro possessore** possessor when the petitioner presents his evidence.

[135]Grotius, *De Jure Belli et Pac.,* Book II, ch. 7 §. 10.

acquisition of property through contract.[136] This conception would find its refutation, if it needed another, in the fact that disposition over property beyond one's lifetime is left unexplained, that the transfer of liabilities in no way can be derived from it, etc. Hegel was the first to conceive succession in its proper significance as the result of the familial bond, and thus intestate succession as the original form.[137] But Hegel's conception, as already noted, needs to be developed in more detail in that this substantial bond likewise includes both the will and the act of the testator, and therefore the latter aspect, to a certain degree and under certain circumstances, is made into its own independent principle of succession. Only in this manner can testamentary succession be understood at all, and it moderates Hegel's exaggerated aversion to testaments. The St. Simonian denial of the law of inheritance is based on the concept, like the more moderated denial of property described above (§. 33), that one can only have property in what he has acquired through his own labor. It is however illogical that despite this the St. Simonians always allow property to exist, even in that which is the mere gift of nature.

---

[136]Kant, *Doctrine of Law*, p. 134.

[137]In the area of positive legal science this happened contemporaneously through others, e.g. Savigny.

APPENDIX: REGARDING THE VALUE OF ROMAN PRIVATE LAW

§. 96. Greatness and Shortcoming of Roman Law

<187> It is a true and now widespread insight that Roman law first and foremost *realized the idea of law* in world history.[138] The significance of this statement is, as we already discussed (Book II [*Principles of Law*], §. 17), a dual one in accordance with the nature of law: the realization of law in both the objective and the subjective sense. Both the pure exclusive validity of positive legal norms without admixture of moral or political motives and the unconditional recognition and preservation of acquired rights is the great character trait which distinguishes the Romans from previous peoples. The struggle to preserve a form of the state considered to be divine was, at least in later times, foreign to them; the struggle to produce an ideal form of state was from the beginning foreign to them. The inviolability of the legal order and of acquired rights are the ground motive of their public condition. This in fact is <188> the origin of the conscious and implemented separation of personal and real rights which we must consider to be the true foundation of a secure private-legal condition (§. 37).

The concept of entitlement (law in the subjective sense, acquired rights) nevertheless manifests itself in a one-sided conceptualization with the Romans, namely as *simple pure entitlement, unpermeated and unmitigated by any duty and higher determining necessity.* Not that the Romans, as with the current natural-law and revolution theory, assumed abstract content-less human rights or that they only attributed to citizens mere rights and no duties: it is everywhere

---

[138] This insight, induced by the great historical investigations of our time, was first expressed with clarity and specificity by Hegel. The earlier period (Herder, Johannes Müller) is far behind him. Despite this, I by no means subscribe to Hegel's further exposition regarding the Roman world epoch. Nor can I find its eternal significance, like Hegel does, in the fact that the opposition of both aspects, the substantial (objective) and the subjective, were expressed in the two classes and their struggle, nor can I find Hegel's ethical verdict regarding the Romans in opposition to the Greeks to be true and justified. Even so, this is not the place to enter further into this discussion.

specific, concrete, established rights as they derive from the nature of the legal institution, the vocation of various positions in life, the purpose of commerce. But measure and restriction in the use of these rights, their dependence on a counter-performance, on the fulfillment of a duty, as likewise ought to proceed from the nature of the legal institution, is unamenable to the Roman conception; the duties exist as an entirely separate matter, beside and outside the rights. In the Roman conception, *law* is a *sphere of the completely absolute (sovereign) action.*

§. 97. One-Sided Focus on Bare Entitlement

This character trait is already often manifest in its *public law*. The consul had the right stemming from the nature of his office to accept votes; viewing this in terms of the described spirit as a right, he might arbitrarily refuse to accept the votes for this person or that. By virtue of their vocation, the senators have the right to vote in extensive speeches, in consequence of which, in accordance with the Roman conception, it is their right before addressing the matter at hand, "to speak about what they wished, as long as they wished." The Decemviri had as supreme ruling authority the right to call new elec- **<189>** toral assemblies and therefore might, as was their right, also decline to do so, by which it came about that they remained in office beyond the lawful term. Even the supremely important institution of censorship as an ethical court of judgment arose only in this manner. In establishing the office of censor, no one thought of an ethical court, but instead the long-omitted wealth estimate and the classification in classes according to this estimate. The estimate was however from then on the right and therefore as everywhere else the pure right of the censors, who therefore in accordance with the free exercise of their right placed anyone in the class they wished, and they would place those who badly managed their farm or poorly groomed their horse, etc., in the poorest class, made them into Aerarii, as they, from a motive of revenge, did to Mamercus Aemilius without any grounds for doing so. The offices were not without any obligation; they were subject to accusation afterward; but the content of the right itself, the manner of its exercise, was not predetermined by this obligation, for which reason any manner of exercise was valid and could not be hindered. It is also to be considered a consequence of this conception that in the case of a violation against one of the Roman classes, the accused would be judged not by those of his own estate (as according to the Germanic principle), nor by an unbiased third-party court, but precisely by the penultimate estate [vorletzten Stande].

In the area of the *law of material things* [Sachenrechts] this principle can manifest itself less obtrusively since property [Eigenthum] by its very nature is a free right, unalloyed by obligation, over a mere passive object. Even so, a closer inspection reveals that here as well peculiar traits are not lacking. Landed property may not be subjected to any tax on earnings; taxes were levied on property in general, and landed property was included in the assize, but a duty on a specific piece of **<190>** land as such and especially on a specific yield from that land (tithes), as found among other peoples earlier and later, is contrary to the Roman concept (Niebuhr). Likewise, the right of the property-owner is not affected by his obligation as debtor; he is liable to the creditor only in his person, not in his material things. Likewise there are no land taxes [Reallasten], ground rents [Grundrenten], etc., because property would thereby be conditioned by fulfillment of a liability. Precisely from this stems the overly strict implementation of the rule "**servitus in faciendo consistere nequit**" [servitudes do not impose positive acts]. Therefore everywhere the right of property-owners as such cannot be accompanied by an obligation, cannot be dependent upon its fulfillment. Furthermore, there is in the ancient civil law no real right to another's thing that would be dependent upon payment of a deposit, like the later **ager vectigalis** and the manifold relations of this sort which from the beginning were developed by the Germanic law. Both ancient institutions of the category of real and personal servitudes, leaving aside their heterogeneity in other respects, have this in common in contrast with later ones, that they are bare unconditioned rights. Finally, there are no real rights limited by time, which thus contain a restriction in themselves, no property which can cease **ex nunc**, no right to another's thing that is not at least for life. The temporal usufruct is, as is the **habitatio**, expressly explained as being more of a factual than a legal nature.[139] The latter admittedly had yet further a general ground in the nature of the case. **<191>**

[139]It also has to do with the fact that usufruct bequeathed to a minor son as legate, thus acquired from the father, depends not upon the life of the son but of the father. To wit, the entitled must have an unrestricted right. For this reason, though, the actual usufruct must be dissolved with **capitis deminutio**, although not the mere factual, temporal usufruct (Justinian, Digest, 4.6.20, de cap. minut.).

The *law of obligation*, on the other hand, took shape entirely in consequence of this principle of pure entitlement. Upon it, namely, is based the actionability of contracts. It is the notion: the only fully justiciable contracts are those which engender a pure unconditioned right, not a right depending on a counterliability [Gegenverbindlichkeit]. The stipulation is such a one: its innermost significance consisted in engendering absolutely unilateral claims, for even when a counter-stipulation is possible, the consequence is only the existence of two entirely independent claims, not a tie of mutual obligation. In the same manner the written contract [Literatkontrakt] only left room for a unilateral claim to a determinate sum of money, since every counter-debt is settled ipso jure. But real contracts [der Realkontrakt] with their peculiar determinations also originate from this. As long as no party has performed, as for instance in an exchange contract, the right is thoroughly permeated by a liability and conditioned by it; anyone asserting a claim had to recognize that counter-performance could only be demanded on the condition of one's own performance; this is not the Roman way of law. But for the one who has fulfilled his obligation, he is no longer liable for anything, he now has a pure entitlement, legal proceedings are therefore now open to him. The consequence of this, however, is the **jus poenitendi**. Since the one who has performed is the pure beneficiary, is completely free of obligation and only as such can be dealt with, he must have the choice either to demand back his own performance or the other. Apart from this he is treated as obligant as well. But there is no injustice in this, in that while the recipient can withdraw [pönitiren] up until the moment of acceptance, can refuse acceptance, therefore it is no less fair that the seller can withdraw up until the counterperformance takes place. Now these four contracts, which are indispensable in daily life and **<192>** can only exist as reciprocal, form an exception: they have as it were the **privilegium** in the Roman legal system. In this as well, by the way, that basic concept is not without influence on the determination as to what degree a counterperformance must be paid should the performance prove impossible by force of circumstances [bei kasueller Unmöglichkeit].

Just so is this character trait the key to the Roman law of the family. That the family here in a manner of speaking maintained itself in patriarchal independence and solidarity, while the power of the father maintained the highest jurisdiction, the right over life and liberty to some extent even to the exclusion of the power of the state, and that what is acquired by the children becomes part of the communal family estate [Familienvermögen] administered by the father, all of this had nothing strange about it, in fact belongs to the period when entitlement of individuals was as yet undeveloped. What is strange is that the position of the father could be asserted entirely arbitrarily, without any higher moderation and duty, that the father, according to his wish, without any restriction by the state, could condemn his son to death or sell him, that he during his lifetime could dispose arbitrarily of the property* acquired by the family, and in similar manner arbitrarily determine succession. It is however no different from senators speaking about whatever they wish as long as they wish, and the wealth estimator putting whoever he wished into the Aerarii. Paternal power therefore by no means is a form of property, which is how one occasionally has sought to solve this phenomenon, but rather familial power, in itself natural for that time, which however was conceived exclusively as mere entitlement unpermeated and undiminished by obligation and therefore certainly gaining a great resemblance to real rights. This also corresponds with the scientific systematic conception of the Roman jurists. They treat the law of the family not as a system of organized rela- <193> tions, marriage, parental relations, etc., but as a system of powers: **potestas**, **manus**, **mancipium**, therefore even guardianship as a **potestas in capite libero**, and marriage, to the degree that it itself does not contain a power (**manus**), as a mere form of acquisition of paternal power.

§. 98. Eternal Value of Roman Law: Steadfastness

We must view the steadfastness [Unverbrüchlichkeit] of positive law, and the steadfastness of entitlement with the implementation attached to it, as eternal legal truth; and in this regard the Romans were rightly characterized as the classical universal-historical people of the law, similar to the Greeks regarding art and the Jews regarding religion. Against this, the concept of pure entitlement incapable of suffering any admixture of duty is by no means a true principle of law, but instead the one-sidedness and imperfection of the Roman condition. Those gruff hearts and inflexibilities which originally sprang from the same source were of course mitigated, even elevated, by later development, but the lack inherent in it from the beginning still remained, *the lack, to wit, of a positive principle of organic formation*, i.e., human life relations taking shape from their higher concepts, as a whole overarching the participants, and in accordance with this allotting those rights and duties in determinate measure and mutual dependence. Germanic law is determined by such a principle. Its institutions, such as shared property, divided property, property reserved for parental use [Altentheil], caretaker administration of the estate [Interimswirthschaft], law of marital property (with or without community of goods) and the like are therefore unassimilable to the Roman standpoint, and regardless of how one judges the value of many of these institutions taken individually, the principle itself, to be able to evoke such and **<194>** similar institutions, is the true one, and in this regard Germanic law stands higher than Roman. With us, then, the Roman law, in accordance with an inner necessity, largely occupied the sphere in which man stands vis-à-vis man without organic connection; where however such a connection existed, particularly with peculiar positions of station, German law has asserted itself.

§. 99. Eternal Value of Roman Law: System in Terms of the Nature of the Case

In still yet another sense does Roman law represent eternal legal truth besides the steadfastness of positive law and the steadfastness of entitlement. Favored by that radical standpoint, Roman legal science in its prime was able to bring the entire content of private-legal relations, particularly regarding property*, regarding relations of possession and transaction, to clear consciousness and to capture it (to stamp it [marquiren]) in accordance with all its aspects. That is to say, what sorts of dealings or legal relations are possible, how they relate to each other, and what decision follows for them on the condition of the determinate legal principles given in their law. Let this serve as an example of what I mean: the distinction of eviction [Entwährung] on the basis of a ground preceding a contract versus a ground succeeding it, the distinction between **impedimentum naturale** (objective hindrance) and **facultas dandi** (subjective incapacity) in the doctrine of **casus**, determinations regarding **mora** according to which no **culpa** is assumed but nevertheless a hindrance of that sort (not the incapacity of the debtor) exempts from the consequences, the fixed limits of various transactions (purchase, deposit, rental) and the demonstration of consequences lying in the nature of each, the development of various estimates regarding compensation in suits of property and other such institutions, delinea- **<195>** tion of considerations and motives regarding property line revisions (**finium regundorum**), etc., etc. To that degree Roman law is *raison écrit* [written reason], i.e., not a *codex of natural law* but a *codex of the nature of the case*. To wit, this development of relations and their decision is, as a rule, the proper one per se, to the degree that the legal principle itself (thus, in the first example, the bindingness of contract according to the content of consensus, etc.) is proper. On the other hand, where the Roman legal principle is false or one-sided, the entire development is of course useless and cannot serve as the standard for other times and conditions, and to the degree that our condition has new peculiar legal principles (law of marital property, agrarian law, etc.), to that degree can the development of the connections given in those life relations not be expected from the Romans but is to be achieved by our own jurisprudence, for which however that Roman development at the least serves as a pattern and example. The distinction between that which itself is a legal principle and that which is the unfolding of the natural material for the principle, i.e., that which is the nature of the case (Book II [*Principles of Law*], §. 13), clears the way for judgment regarding Roman law which even with the fullest recognition of its value is nevertheless free of all preferential treatment and is fully compatible with the highest esteem and cultivation of Germanic legal elements. For instance, I am, as my exposition of the relevant material everywhere indicates, far from recognizing the Roman law of obligation (to the degree that it is constructed on the basis of restricted actionability), Roman regulations regarding the law of marital property (dowry system, exclusion by relatives of spouses from all inheritance) or paternal power, etc., as *true legal* (ethical) *principles*, although on the other hand I recognize the treatment of the law of obligation (eviction [Eviktion], **<196> casus**, **mora**, **culpa**, Aedilian edict, etc.) as the *true revealed nature of the case.*

This revelation of the nature of the case is however something entirely different and deeper than the *mere intellectual consistency* [Verstandeskonsequenz] emphasized by Hegel as the only and in fact quite equivocal advantage of Roman law. The Romans' intellectual consistency is of course also an indispensable medium for applying legal principles to the matters of life in a proper and harmonious manner, for which reason it generally is likewise an example for all jurisprudence, even though it occasionally, especially in the system of **strictum jus**, breaks loose from actual needs of life and borders on hair-splitting. It is only through this consistency that the Romans were able to complete their law as an implemented system, closed in itself, although with the parts calibrated in terms of each other. But this mere consistency in itself would not have assured Roman legal science of its universal-historical power, were it not supported by the energetic concrete observance and valuation of life relations and commercial connections. The nature of the case (i.e., the connections and requirements inherent in factual life relations) stands in profound relation to the law-ideas themselves (Book I [*Philosophical Foundations*], §. 5); in fact, it is none other than the *purpose* (τέλος) *of life relations* which we have assigned as the principle of legal philosophy, only in subordinate fashion, that is to say it does not refer to the *highest final* goal, thus the actual ethical ideas of the institution, but, assuming this to be given in positive law, to the *intermediate* goals. The Roman jurists therefore are the most complete legal philosophers in this sphere, although for the highest sphere, the profoundest ethical and social principles of law, they are not that in the least.

Should one consider the value of Roman law to lie in the complete exposition of law-ideas rather than in the complete **<197>** exposition of the nature of the case, then one runs the risk of harming national legal development to its benefit. On the other hand, should one consider that value to lie in logical consistency, systematic completion, antique simplicity, that which is commonly understood as the scientific exemplariness of Roman law, thus only the *formal* aspect of the method of treatment, one thereby fails to appreciate that Roman law also contains a plethora of outstanding *material* decisions just as true for our conditions as for Roman. At this point it is idle to ask whether nevertheless it would have been more felicitous if Roman law had not formally been received in Germany but had only served as a pattern for free imitation. This having happened, we do not wish to rejoice in its possession merely as a legal-scientific *strength* but also as a legal-scientific *treasure*, and this will not keep the life-appreciation of the nation and the present, wherever such is established, from being brought to validity and authentication in the law. An ejection of Roman legal material from our life is as little possible as it is desirable. Just as the English people grew from Romans and Germans into a single people, its speech grew from a twofold stock into one speech; in a similar manner our law in Germany will always bear the imprint of its double descent in itself, and when in accordance with Dahlmann's true remark that mixtures of peoples [Völkermischungen] of that sort by no means tend to yield the worst products, why should the same not hold true for mixtures of law? The task, however, to assign to each its proper and beneficial portion and to promote their inner unification in legal consciousness as well as legal conditions, cannot be solved in the area of general reflection but only for each legal institution in accordance with its particular requirement. An undeniable fact is that we have entered a period in which, to a degree which has not been seen earlier, the legal profession [Juristenstand] is filled with the **<198>** knowledge of German law and in consequence as well with its spirit and the measure of its judgment. That hereby the German element must ever more attain the greater extension coming to it is a surely inevitable consequence and one of the best hopes of the national condition (Bluntschli). The proponents of the doctrine which first brought the coherence of law and people and thereby the national significance of law to scientific consciousness cannot and will not greet this other than with joy, and work for its fulfillment each according to vocation and gift. *Historical* direction and *national* direction are so little in contradiction that they much rather mutually condition each other, and when the one combats the other, it only misunderstands itself.

WORKS CITED BY STAHL

Acts, Book of. Cited on page 46.

Aquinas, St. Thomas. *Summa theologiae.* Various editions. Cited on page 139.

Aristotle, *Politics.* Various editions. Cited on page 45.

Bull. magn. [further information unavailable]. Cited on page 120.

Carpzov, Benedict. *Jurisprudentia ecclesiastica seu consistorialis....* 1649 and many editions thereafter. Cited on page 143.

Considerant, V. *Destinée Sociale.* Paris: Phalange, 1837–1844. Cited on page 62.

Eichhorn, Karl Friedrich. *Principles of the the Ecclesiastical Law of the Catholic and Protestant Religious Party in Germany* [Grundsätze des Kirchenrechts der katholischen und der evangelischen Religionspartei in Deutschland]. Göttingen. Vandenhoeck und Ruprecht, 1831–1833. Cited on page 129.

Gans, Eduard. *Foundation of Possession* [Ueber die Grundlage des Besitzes: eine Duplik]. Berlin: Veit, 1839. Cited on page 90.

—. *Universal-Historical Development of the Law of Succession* [Das Erbrecht in weltgeschichtlicher Entwicklung: eine Abhandlung der Universalrechtsgeschichte]. Berlin: 1824. Cited on page 180.

Gerlach, Otto von. *Regarding the Current Shape of Marriage Law* [Ueber die heutige Gestalt des Eherechts]. Second edition. Berlin: Oehmigke, 1842. Cited on page 142.

Gros, Karl Heinrich. *Textbook of Philosophical Legal Science or of Natural Law* [Lehrbuch der philosophischen Rechtswissenschaft oder des Naturrechts]. Stuttgart: 1829. Cited on page 103.

Grotius, Hugo. *De Jure Belli et Pacis* [The Law of War and Peace]. 1625. Cited on page 34, 164, 185.

Harless, Gottlieb Christoph Adolf von (ed.). *Journal for Protestantism and Church* [Zeitschrift für Protestantismus und Kirche]. Erlangen: A. Deichert. Cited on page 156.

Hegel, G. W. F. *Encyclopedia of Philosophical Sciences* [Encyklopädie der philosophischen Wissenschaften]. Unspecified edition. Cited on page 117.

—. *Lectures on the Philosophy of History* [Vorlesungen über die Geschichte der Philosophie]. Aalten: WordBridge Publishing, 2011 [1833]. Cited on page 28.

—. *Philosophy of Law* [Grundlinien der Philosophie des Rechts]. Berlin: Nicolaische Buchhandlung, 1821. Cited on pages 5, 11, 57, 101, 109, 139, 150, 178.

d'Hericourt du Vatier, Louis. *The Ecclesiastical Laws of France* [Les Lois Ecclesiastiques de France]. Paris: 1721. Cited on page 125.

Hüttner, Johann Christian. Translation of William Jones, *Institutes of Hindu law; or, the Ordinances of Menu, according to the gloss of Cullúca: comprising the Indian system of duties, religious and civil* [1796]. Weimar, 1797. Cited on page 67.

Kant, Immanuel. *Metaphysical Elements of the Doctrine of Law* [Metaphysische anfangsgründe der Rechtslehre]. Königsberg: bey Friedrich Nicolovius, 1797. Cited on page 25, 65, 104, 105 109, 145, 164, 185.

Koch, Christian Friedrich. *Das Recht der Forderungen nach gemeinem und nach preußischem Rechte* [The Law of Obligations according to the Common and the Prussian Law], 3 volumes. Breslau: 1836–1843. Cited on page 108.

Justinian, *Corpus Iuris Civilis,* Novel 117. Cited on page 143.

Justinian, *Digest,* 4.6.20, de cap. minut. Cited on page 191.

—, l. 12 §. 1 de adqu. vel amitt. poss. (41.2). Cited on page 86.

—, *Digest,* l. 39. §. 1, de jure dot., j. de adopt. Cited on page 120.

Lauterbach, Wolfgang Adam. *Collegium Pandectarum theoretico-practicum.* 3 volumes. Tubingae: 1714–25. Cited on page 143.

Luther, Martin. *Complete Writings* [Sämtliche Schriften], vol. X. Edited by Johann Georg Walch. Halle: 1739–1753. Cited on pages 131, 145.

Pfordten, Ludwig Karl von der. *Treatises from the Laws of the Pandects* [Abhandlungen aus dem Pandektenrechte]. Erlangen: 1840. Cited on page 108.

Plato. *The Laws.* Various editions. Cited on page 50.

Proudhon, Pierre Joseph. *What is Property?* [Qu'est-ce que la propriété?]. Nouvelle éd. Paris: Marpon-Flammarion, 1841. Cited on page 61.

Puchta, Georg Friedrich. *Leaflets for Questions of the Day* [Fliegende Blätter: Beiträge zu den Fragen des Tages], I. Berlin: 1843. Cited on pages 142, 151.

Savigny, Friedrich Carl von. *Representation of the Reform Undertaken in the Prussian Divorce Laws* [Darstellung der in den Preußischen Gesetzen über die Ehescheidung unternommenen Reform]. Berlin: Veit, 1844. Cited on pages 142, 144, 145, 151.

—. *The Right of Possession* [Das Recht des Besitzes : Eine civilistische Abhandlung]. Gießen : Heyer, 1806. Cited on page 89.

—. *System of the Modern Roman Law* [Pand., a.k.a. System des heutigen Römischen Rechts]. Leipzig : Veit, 1840. Cited on page 101.

Schelling, Friedrich Wilhelm Joseph von. *On the Relation of the Real and the Ideal in Nature* [Ueber das Verhältniß des Realen und Idealen in der Natur, oder

Entwicklung der ersten Grundsätze der Naturphilosophie an den Principien der Schwere und des Lichts]. Hamburg: Perthes, 1806. Cited on page 117.

Stahl, F. J. *Ancient Roman Law of Accusation* [Ueber das ältere Römische Klagenrecht]. München: 1827. Cited on page 86.

—. *The Catholic Refutations* [Die katholischen Widerlegungen: eine Begleitungsschrift zur 4. Aufl. meiner Vorträge über den Protestantismus als politisches Princip]. Berlin: 1854. Cited on page 174.

—. *The Church Constitution According to the Doctrine and Law of Protestants* [Die Kirchenverfassung nach Lehre und Recht der Protestanten]. Erlangen: T. Bläsing, 1840. Cited on page 130.

—. *The Philosophy of Law According to the Historical Perspective: Volume II: Christian Doctrine of Law and State* (Heidelberg: J. C. B. Mohr, 1833). Cited on p. 117.

—. *The Philosophy of Law: Volume I: The History of Legal Philosophy* [Die Philosophie des Rechts: Bd. 1: Geschichte der Rechtsphilosophie]. Third Edition. Heidelberg: Mohr, 1854. Cited on pages 28, 57; second edition, pp. 10, 11.

—. *The Philosophy of Law: Volume II: The Doctrine of Law and State on the Basis of the Christian World-View* [Rechts- und Staatslehre auf der Grundlage christlicher Weltanschauung]. Third edition. Heidelberg : Mohr, 1854. Cited on the following pages:

Book I [*Philosophical Foundations*]: 3, 13, 14, 19, 21, 108, 111, 119, 122, 166, 190, 191, 197

Book II [*Principles of Law*]: 4, 6, 8, 34, 36, 37, 49, 53, 78, 80, 84, 98, 99, 103, 106, 111, 114, 144, 145, 147, 148, 159, 162, 163, 181, 187, 196

Book IV [*Doctrine of State & the Principles of State Law*]: 51, 59

—. *Protestantism as a Political Principle* [Der Protestantismus als politisches Princip]. Second unrevised edition. Berlin: Schultze, 1853. Cited on page 174.

—. *Parliamentary Speeches* [Parlamentarische Reden]. Ed. J. P. M. Treuherz. Berlin: Verlag von Hermann Hollstein, 1856. Cited on p. 164.

—. *Seventeen Parliamentary Speeches and Three Lectures* [Siebzehn parlamentarische Reden und drei Vorträge]. Berlin: Hertz, 1862. Cited on p. 17.

—. *Speeches* [Reden]. Berlin: Hertz, 1850. Cited on p. 32.

Steffens, Heinrich. *Anthropology* [Anthropologie]. Breslau: Josef Max, 1822. Cited on page 118.

Stein, Lorenz von. *Socialism and Communism in Contemporary France* [Der Socialismus und Communismus des heutigen Frankreichs]. Leipzig: Wigand, 1842. Cited on page 62.

Tancred., ed. Wund. [further information unavailable]. Cited on page 119.

Theiner, Johannes A.: Variae doctorum catholicorum opiniones de jure statuendi impedimenta matrimonium dirimentia: dissertatio canonica. Breslau: 1824. Cited on page 126

Thomasius, Christian. *Institutions of Divine Jurisprudence, in which the Foundations of Natural Law are Clearly Demonstrated According to the Principles of the Illustrious Pufendorf* [Institutionum jurisprudentiae divinae libri tres : in quibus fundamenta juris naturalis secundum hypotheses illustris Pufendorffii perspicus demonstrantur ... Editio septima porioribus multo correctior, ... acc. Halae Magdeburgicae]: Salfeld, 1730. Cited on page 164.

Walter, *Archiv für das Kriminalrecht*, vol. IV [further information unavailable]. Cited on page 8.

Walter, Ferdinand. *Textbook of Canon Law* [Lehrbuch des Kirchenrechts: aus den älteren und neueren Quellen bearbeitet]. Second edition (many other editions available). Bonn: Marcus, Büschler, 1823. Cited on page 123.

Wiese, Georg Walter Vincent von. *Textbook of Ecclesiastical Law* [Handbuch des gemeinen in Teutschland üblichen Kirchenrechts als Commentar über seine Grundsätze desselben]. Vol. III. Leipzig: 1804. Cited on page 145.

ROMAN LEGAL TERMS

N.B.: Many of these terms may be referenced in William Smith, *A Dictionary of Greek and Roman Antiquities.*[140]

[140] URL: https://tinyurl.com/48au6euy

INDEX

N.B.: The page numbers below refer to the numbering of the original edition.

www.ingramcontent.com/pod-product-compliance
Ingram Content Group UK Ltd.
Pitfield, Milton Keynes, MK11 3LW, UK
UKHW021908190726
13853UKWH00002B/568